# Art of Imbue

with narrative by
## Luke Reynods

Written and created by Luke Reynolds
Book production by Luke Reynolds
Cover design and layouts by Luke Reynolds

Front cover illustrations by Andrew Hyska, Christopher Moeller, Chris Smith, and Jason Swope
Back cover illustrations by Nicole Hansche, Andrew Hyska, Christopher Moeller, Chris Smith, and Jason Swope
Illustrations by Nicole Hansche can be found on pages 4, 8-9
Illustrations by Andrew Hyska can be found on pages 5, 12-13
Illustrations by Christopher Moeller can be found on pages 5, 16-17
Illustrations by Luke Reynolds can be found on pages 6, 12, 24, 27 - 31
Illustrations by Chris Smith can be found on pages 4, 6-7
Illustrations by Jason Swope can be found on pages 5, 14-15, 18-26, 32-36
Illustrations by Hillary Wilson can be found on pages 4, 10-11

# Introduction

Hello reader. My name is Luke Reynolds. I am the founder and owner of Cryptiquest and the creator and author of Imbue. This book features the artwork created for Imbue and some personal stories related to the project.

This book was created as a reward for backers who helped fund the *Imbue Storycrafting Game* Kickstarter campaign. Imbue is a roleplaying game that includes mechanisms for crafting custom content. The *Introduction to Imbue Storycrafting Game* was published in 2016. You can learn more by visiting the website at: http://imbue.cryptiquest.com

---

# The Artists

### Nicole Hansche - Main Image 1

I came across the work of Nicole while searching DeviantArt for talent. I really loved her use of bold colors and her vision for balancing masculinity and femininity. She was the first artist I worked with outside of my circle of contacts and it was a wonderful experience. Nicole is a great artist to work with and I hope to do so again.

### Andrew Hyska - Main Image 3

Andrew and I have known each other for ages though it's only been just recently that we have gotten to know each other. As a visual artist he tends to execute designs with whatever medium is at his fingertips, including highlighters, sticky notes, and ball point pens. I like his style and hope to work with him again.

### Christopher Moeller - Main Image 5

Christopher is an industry giant who I found while searching local artists. I was surprised by his ability to understand my pseudoscience-magic babbling. Normally I struggle to convey the half-formed visions from my head to artists and they are understandably confused but Christopher could fill in the blanks and relay back to me the complete picture. And he has such a talent for rendering a complicated scene into a beautifully concise masterpiece. I'd be honored to commission him again in the future.

### Chris Smith - Cover Image

Chris and I have overlapping social circles. I've always been a huge fan of his work and was thrilled when an opportunity came up to commission him. I remember meeting at his house to discuss the piece. There was a wicked storm brewing outside and the power went out a couple of times during the meeting. Luckily the house didn't blow down and we could hash out the direction and style of the cover art. I really hope to commission him again in the future.

### Jason Swope - Main Image 4 and Various Pieces

Jason and I are good friends and housemates. I'm extremely lucky to be close to such a great talent. Often I can give him a sketch or a visual problem and he'll tease at it until the solution becomes clear. And sometimes I can say "here's a summary and some references, can you give me an illustration?" and he'll produce something magical. I have the most fun taking Jason's artwork and incorporating it into media (books, videos, etc.).

### Hillary Wilson - Main Image 2

I discovered the work of Hillary in a google search for fantasy landscape artists. I think it's safe to say that anyone looking at her work is immediately transfixed and teleported into some magical place. Working with her was a great experience as she made everything easy. I look forward to working with her again.

### Luke Reynolds - Various Pieces

This is me, the author of the book you are reading and the creator, author, and producer of the Imbue project (and owner and founder of Cryptiquest, LLC). Sometimes, in a pinch, I also create artwork. It's not my favorite thing to do and it's not my wheelhouse but sometimes it's necessary. At times, I'll whip up a sketch in order to illustrate my ideas and then hand them off to an artist as a reference and at other times my sketches are either "good enough" or "will have to do" (due to time or budget constraints). I have a feeling that you will be able to tell which art piece goes into which category. Like all the others, I hope to work with myself again in the future!

# Main Images

## Cover Piece by Chris Smith

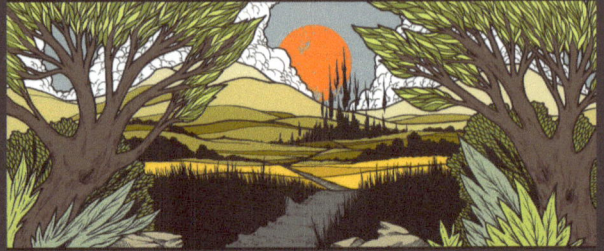

For the cover I wanted something cinematic, something that had mystery and invitation. The idea was that the viewer would look at a settlement far off in the distance which had floating skyscrapers. There were to be vast, serene plains between the settlement and the viewer, who was standing just inside the Wilds.

I think Chris was confused when I first came to him with this request. RPG covers, especially a landscape, has the connotation of a fantasy painting - which is not at all his style. But what I had envisioned was something along the lines of 70s prog-rock-illustration meets cel-shaded-anime, almost like it was drawn in Illustrator, Flash, or some other vector-based program. I also wanted a golden color to be the main fixture in the scheme. We looked at some of his previous work until I pointed to some of his color block artwork. And then he understood what I was going for.

I gave him a crude sketch for framing and he was able to translate that into a thumbnail that eventually became the cover photo.

I was completely blown away when I saw the final art piece and was especially impressed when I found out that it was done by hand. There's absolutely nothing wrong with digital work, but there's something about not having an "undo" button that makes me appreciate manual work even more.

## Chapter 1
## by Nicole Hansche

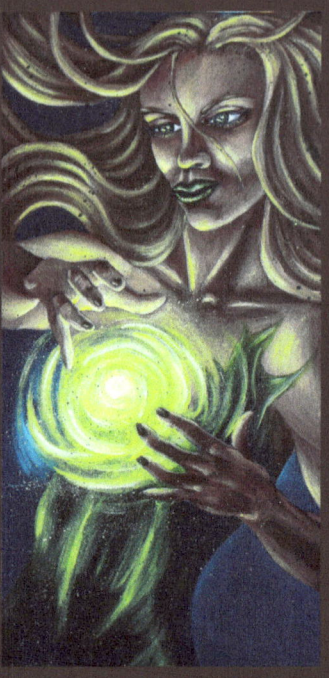

Nicole was the first commissioned artist outside of my social circle. I was fortunate since she was so patient with my inexperience and we forged a healthy partnership. And I was also fortunate as far as talent goes, since she delivered exactly what I asked for. I'm especially enamored by the motion of the hair and the hands surrounding the ball of energy being conjured.

## Chapter 2
## by Hillary Wilson

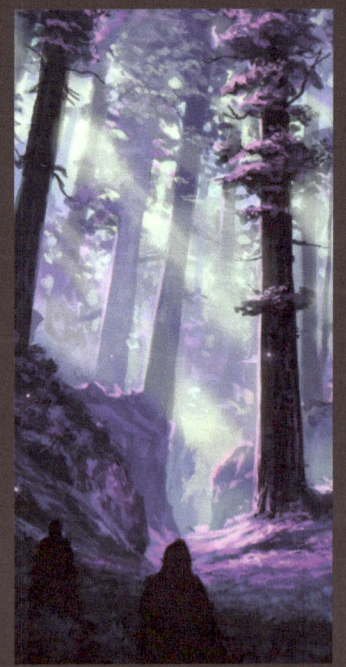

Hillary is another artist outside my circle and was easy to work with. I requested a purple and gray forest with large, flat boulders and some explorers in the foreground and I got that back in the most beautiful way anyone could imagine. I love this piece so much that I use it as my phone's background image.

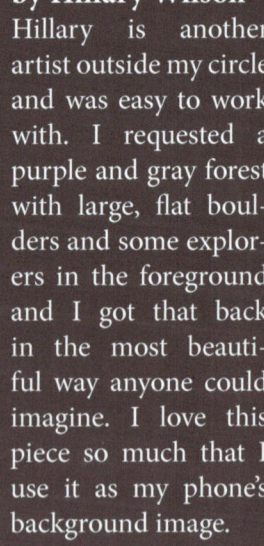

## Chapter 3
## by Andrew Hyska

This was the last big piece I commissioned. I had vetted four different artists for this piece over a 10-month span but for one reason or another they each fell through. Andrew was my hero. He came through at the last hour and really worked on getting the detail of the clothing to match my specifications.

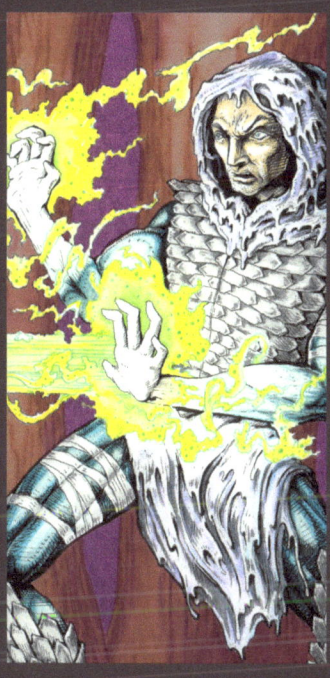

## Chapter 5 by Christopher Moeller

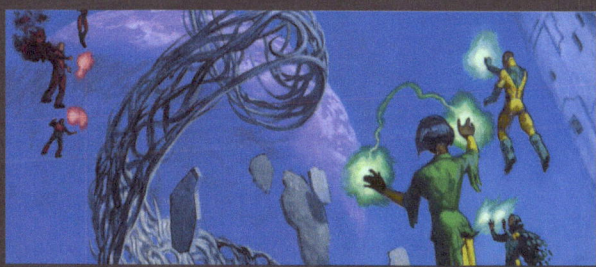

Christopher was another artist outside of my social circle. His reputation as an industry giant was intimidating but he turned out to be one of the nicest people ever. For this piece, I sent him a two-paragraph narrative of the scene, assuming he'd be able to mentally fly around the scene and visualize the best way to convey such a complicated idea. It may not seem very complicated now by looking at the image but remember that before this image existed, there was only a two-paragraph narrative. That's the magic of talent like Christopher, turning the complicated into a concise work of beauty.

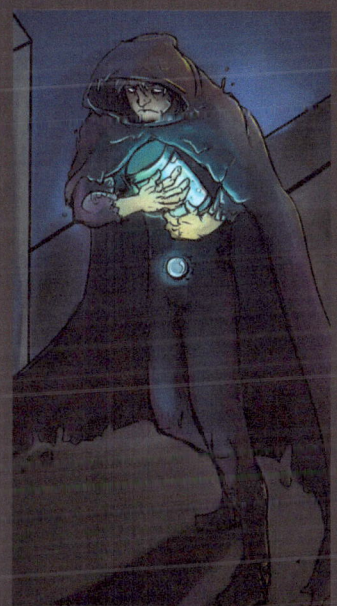

## Chapter 4
## by Jason Swope

Jason and I met in college and have grown close. He's a good collaborator and I really like his art style. He's helped me out of some design jams.

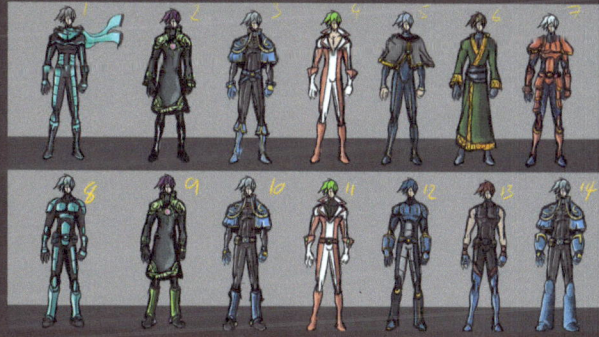

For instance, he was integral in designing a visual solution for how clothing could work. I have a specific understanding of how the fictional technology used to create clothing works in Imbue but not how the clothes would look or the fashions that would stem from such technology. Jason came up with the following sketches to toy around with designs until we came to a consensus on what seemed to work/look best.

The drip cape in the art piece is another great example of design solutions Jason has come up with the in-setting technical restrictions I've imposed.

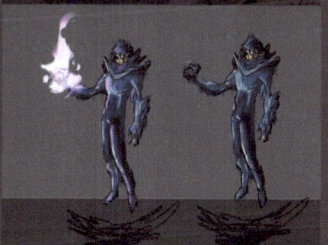

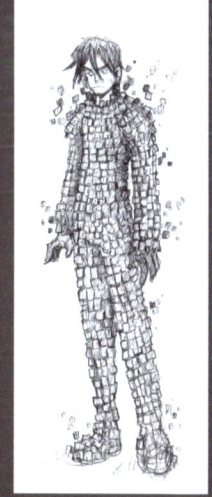

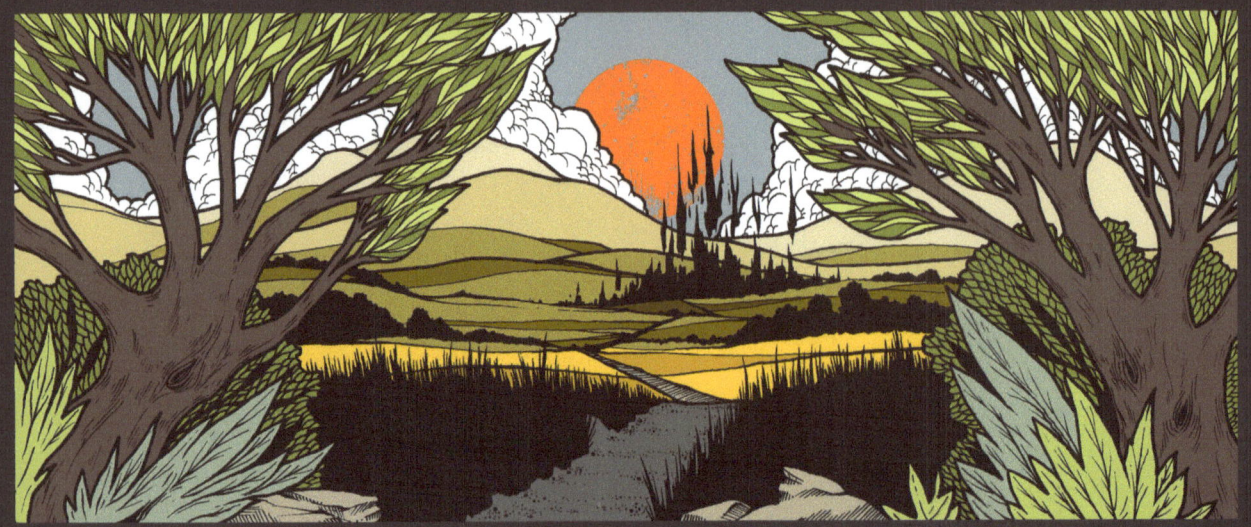

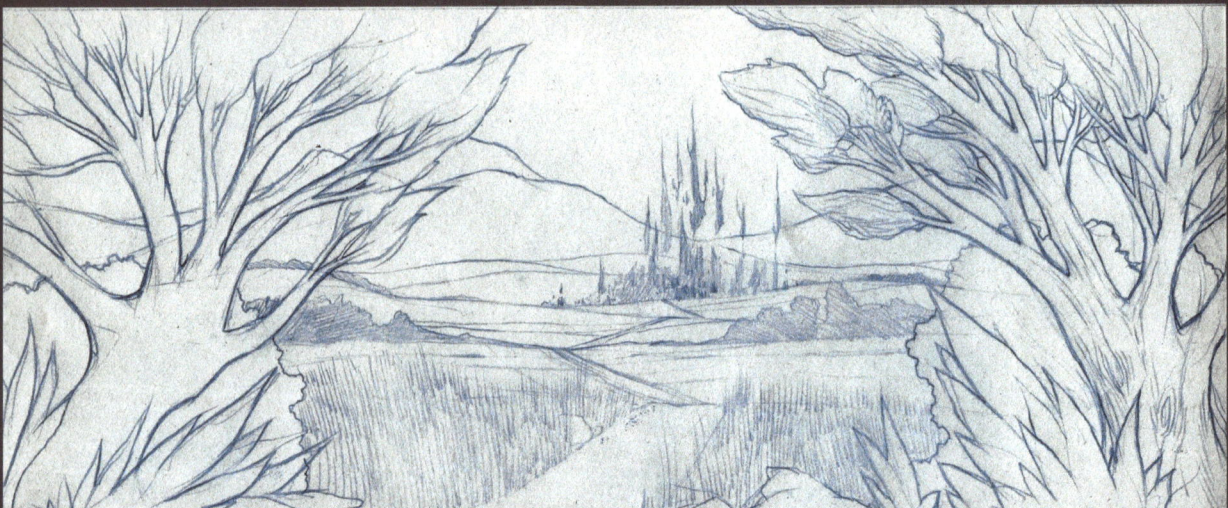

Chris Smith sketch

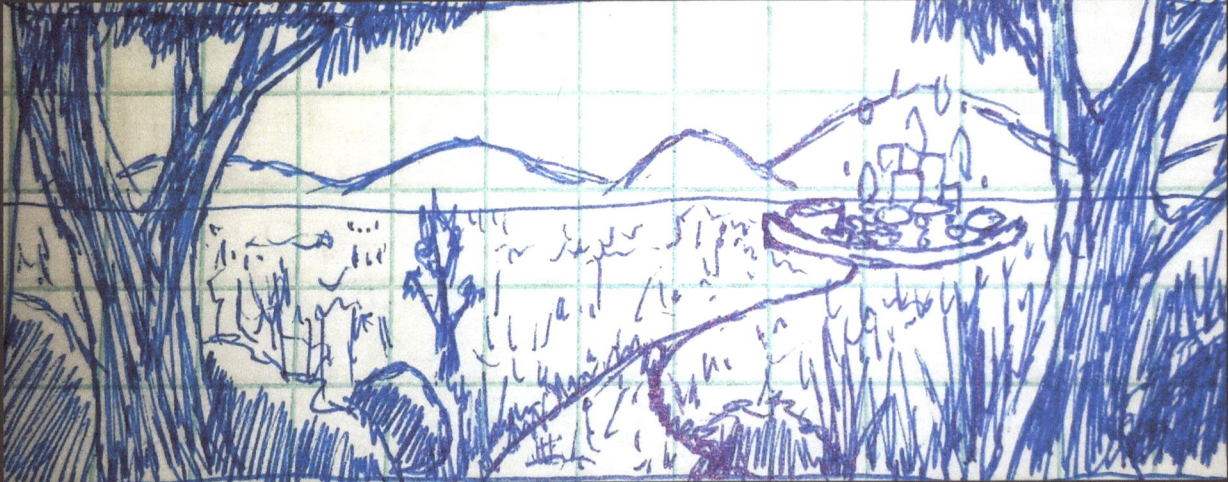

Luke Reynolds sketch

6

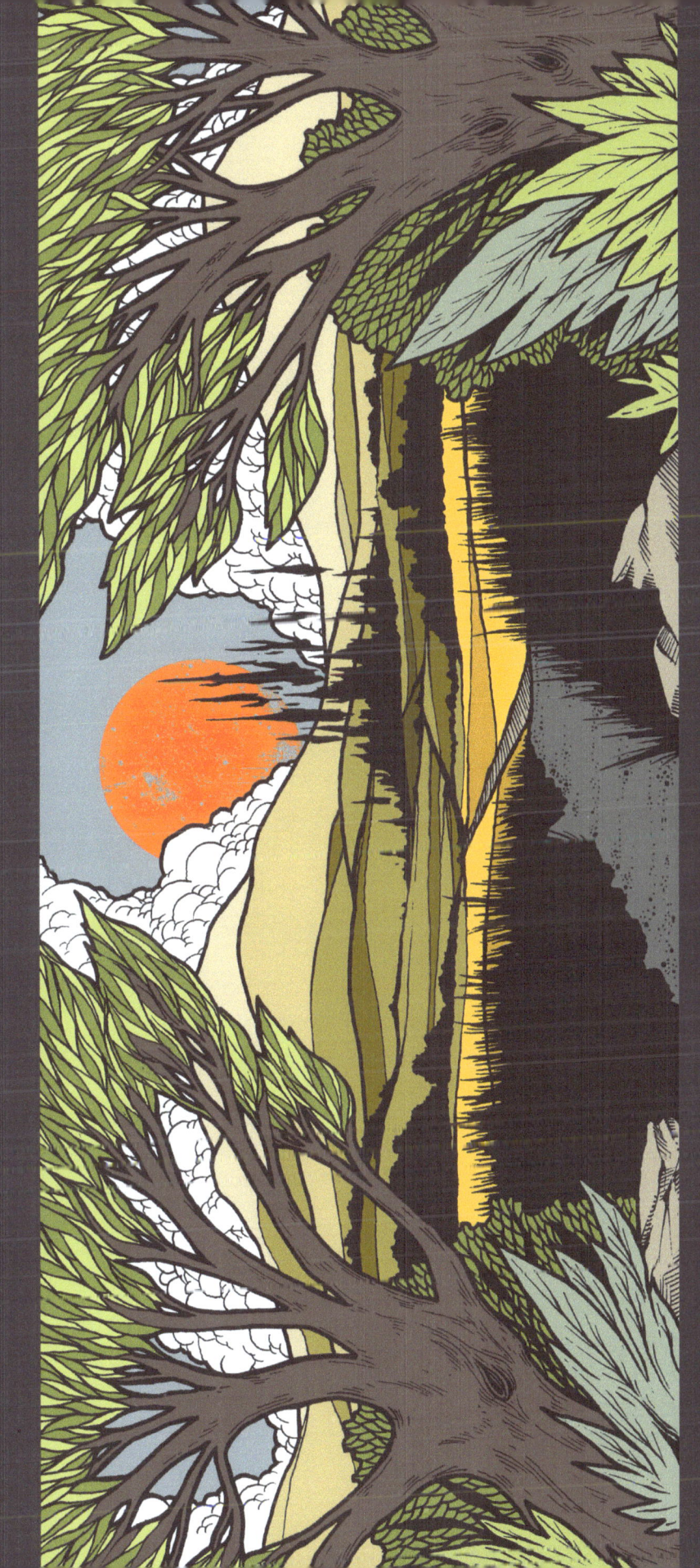

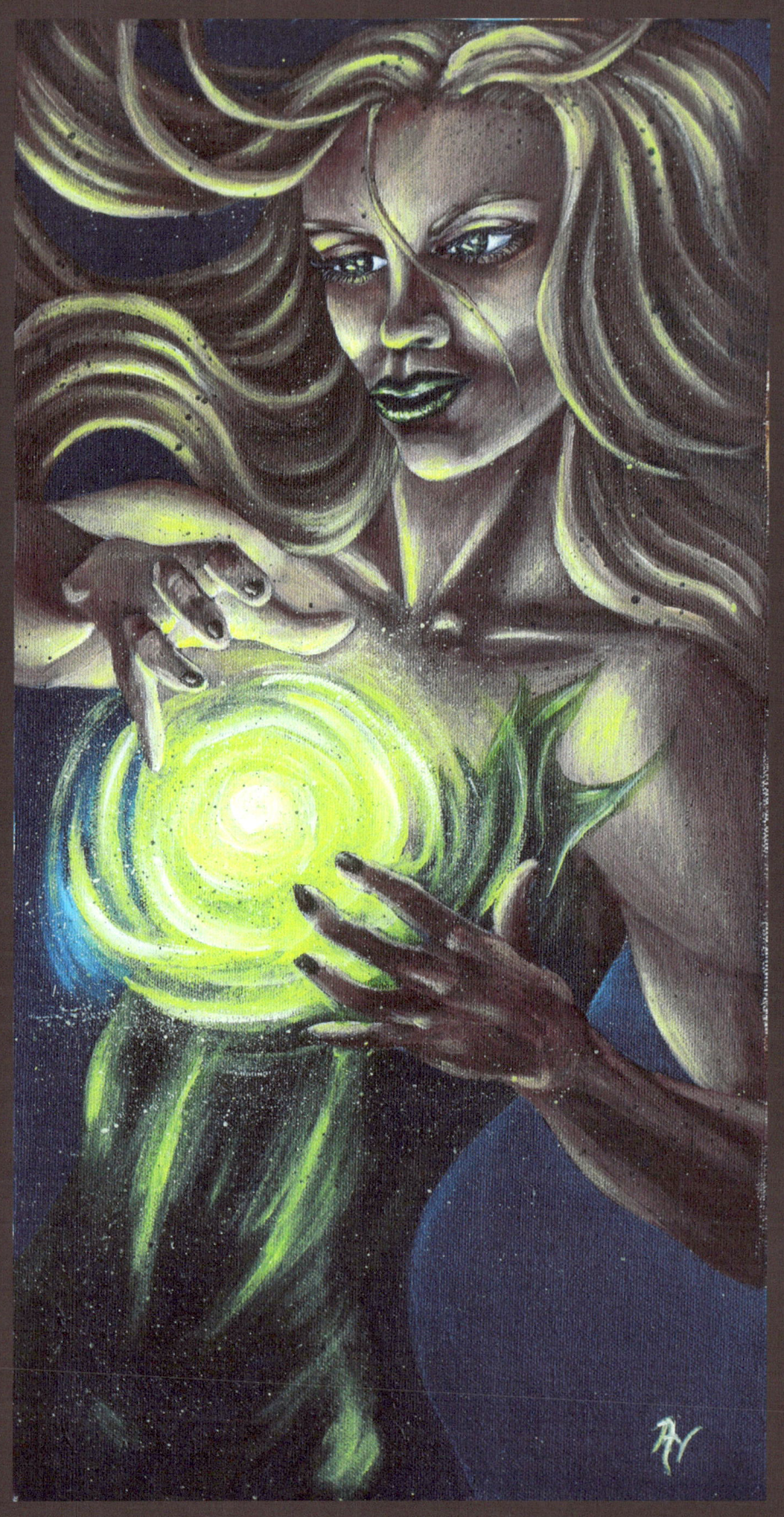

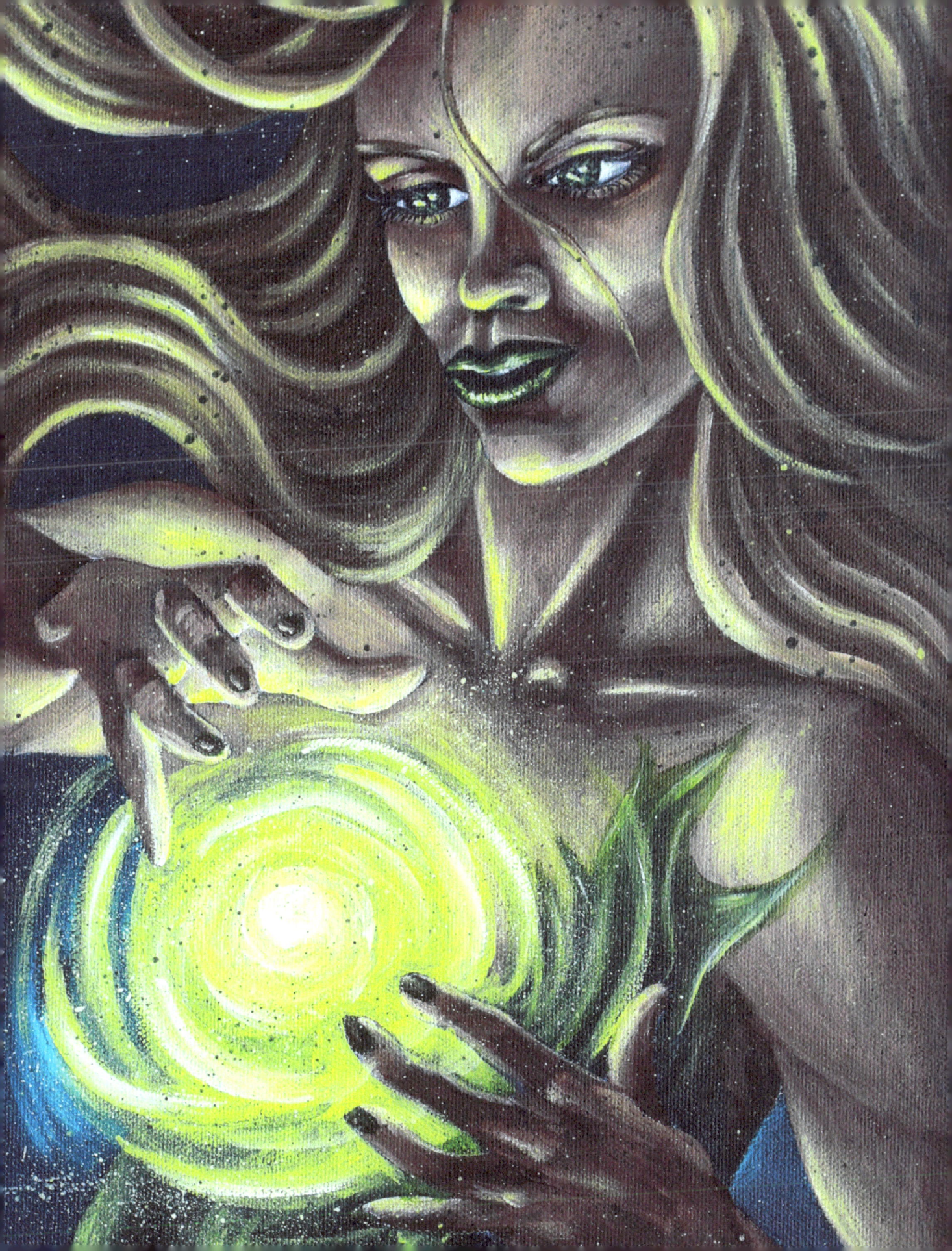

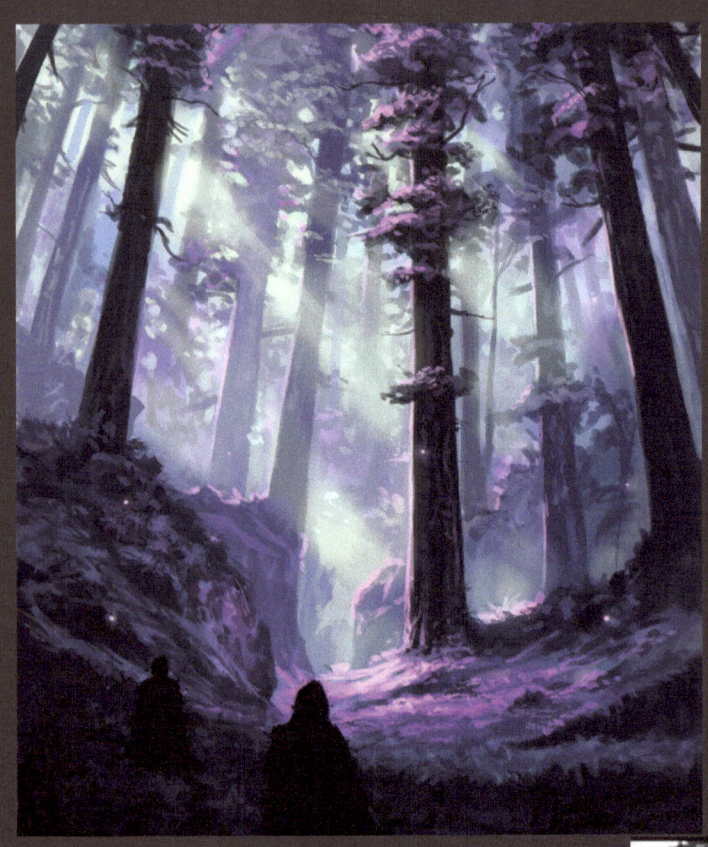

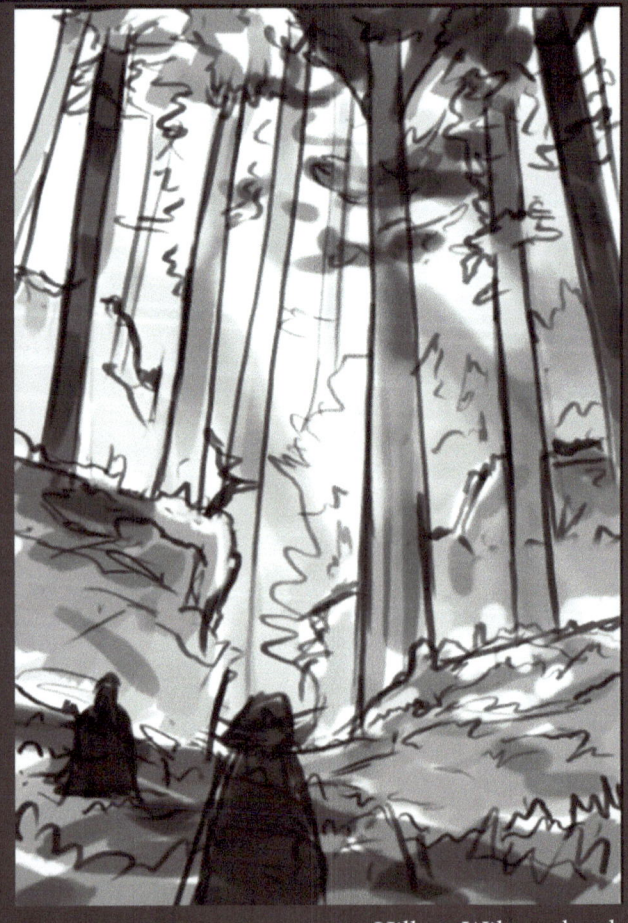

Hillary Wilson sketch

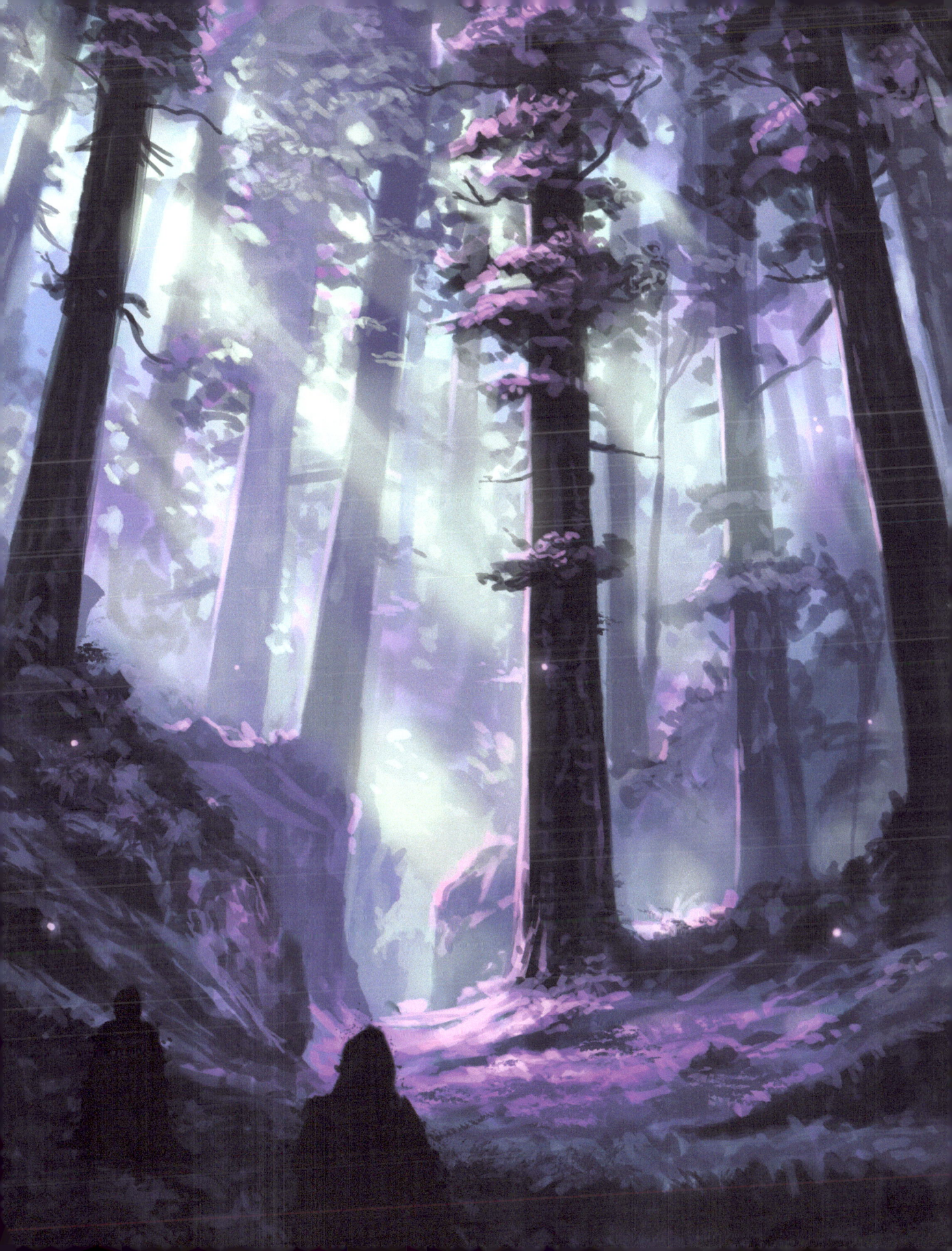

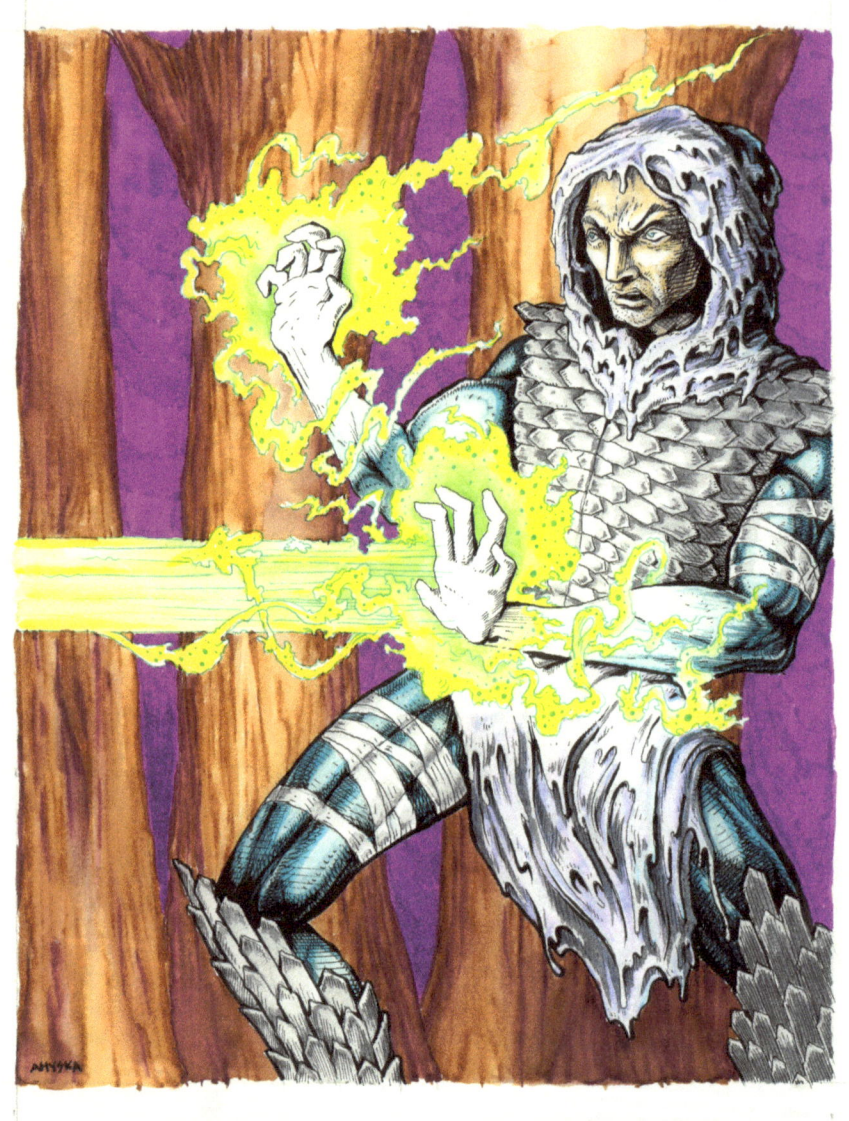

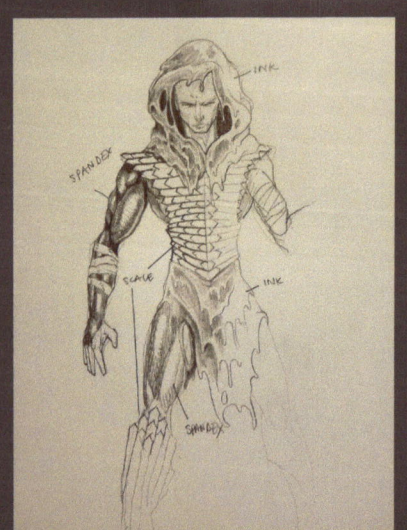

Andrew Hyska sketch

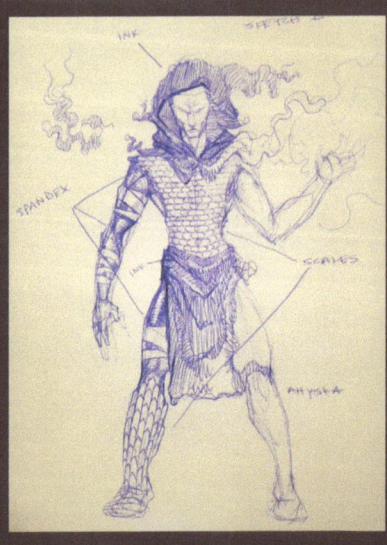

Andrew Hyska sketch

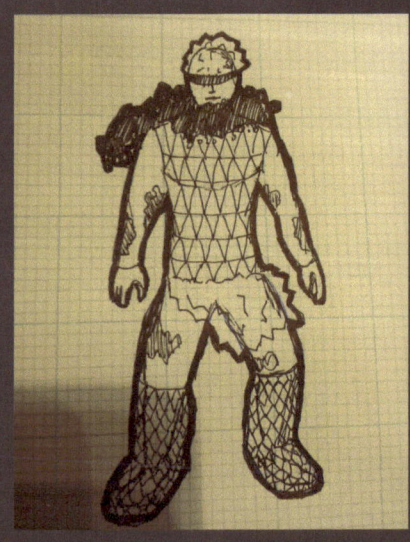

Luke Reynolds sketch

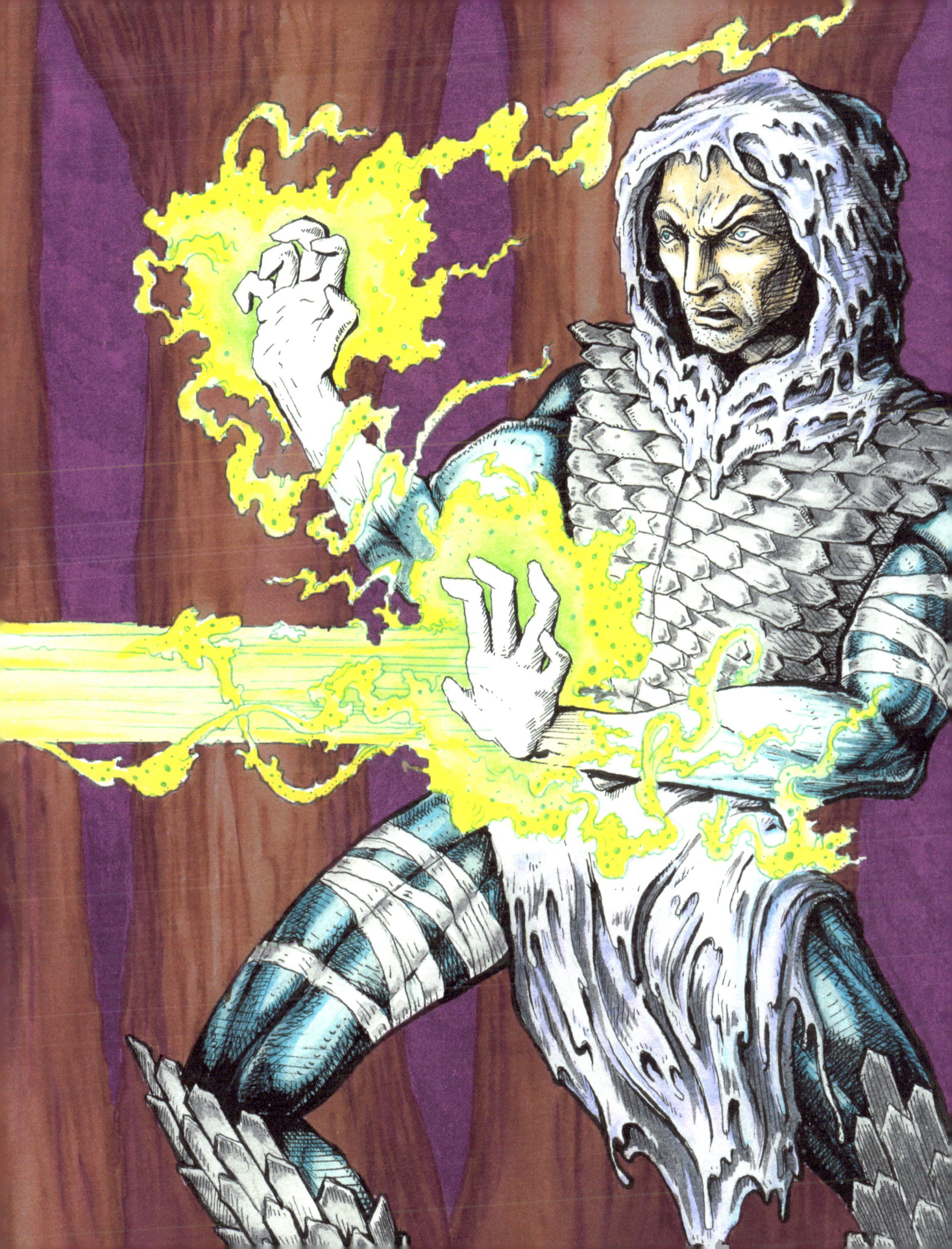

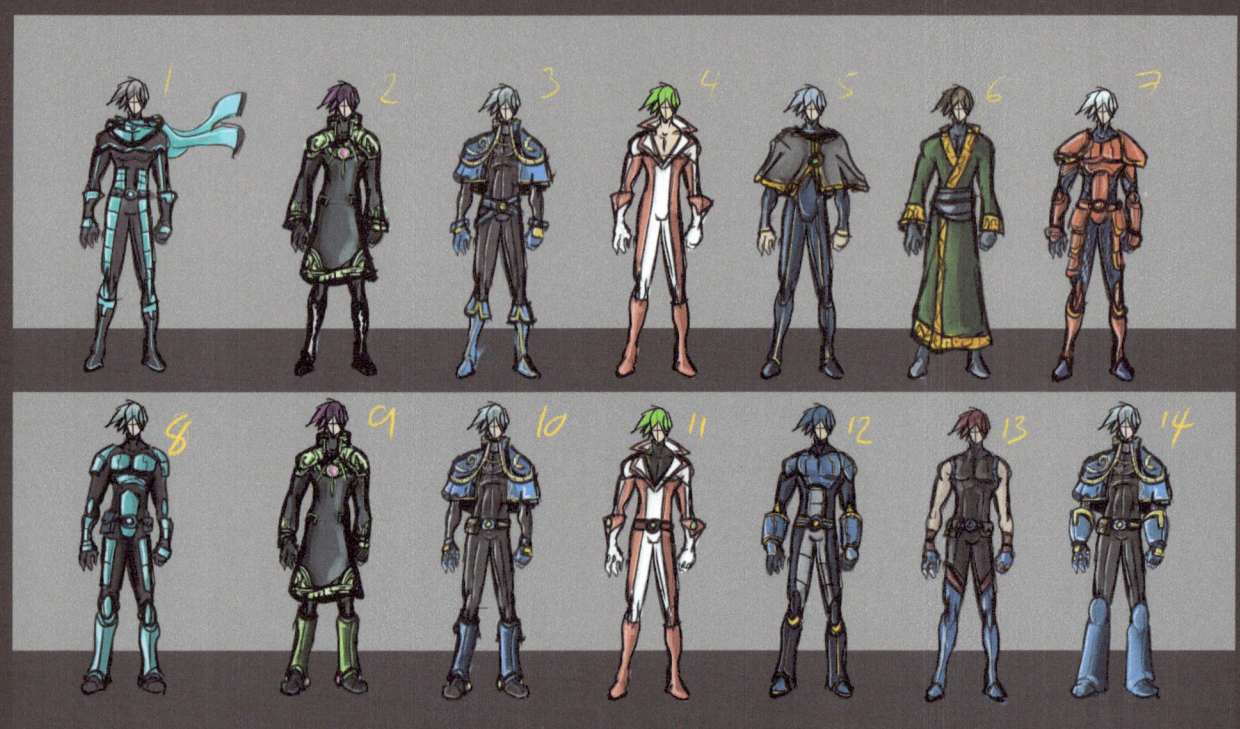

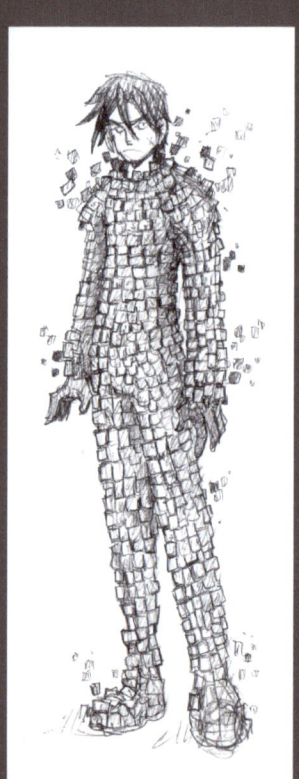

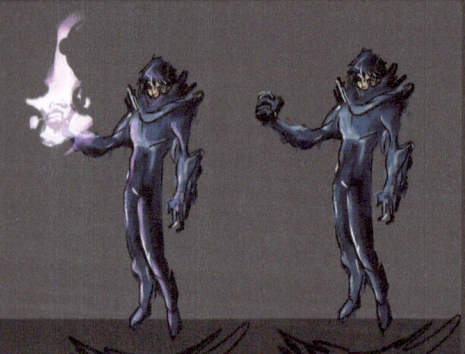

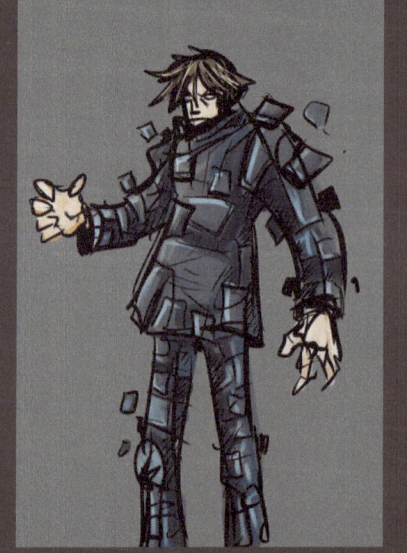

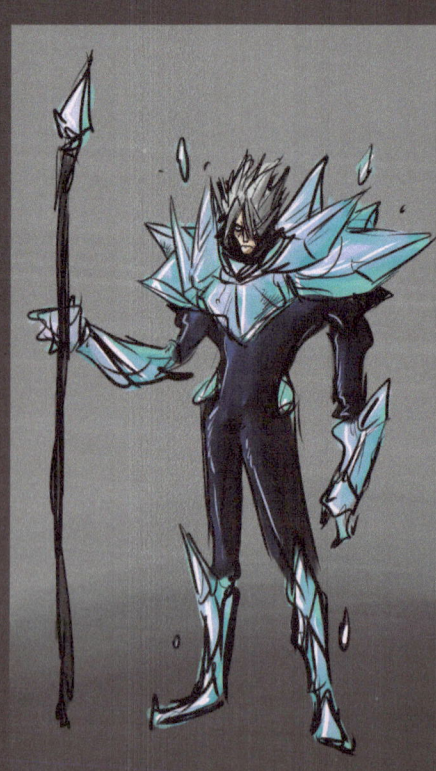

Concept art by Jason Swope

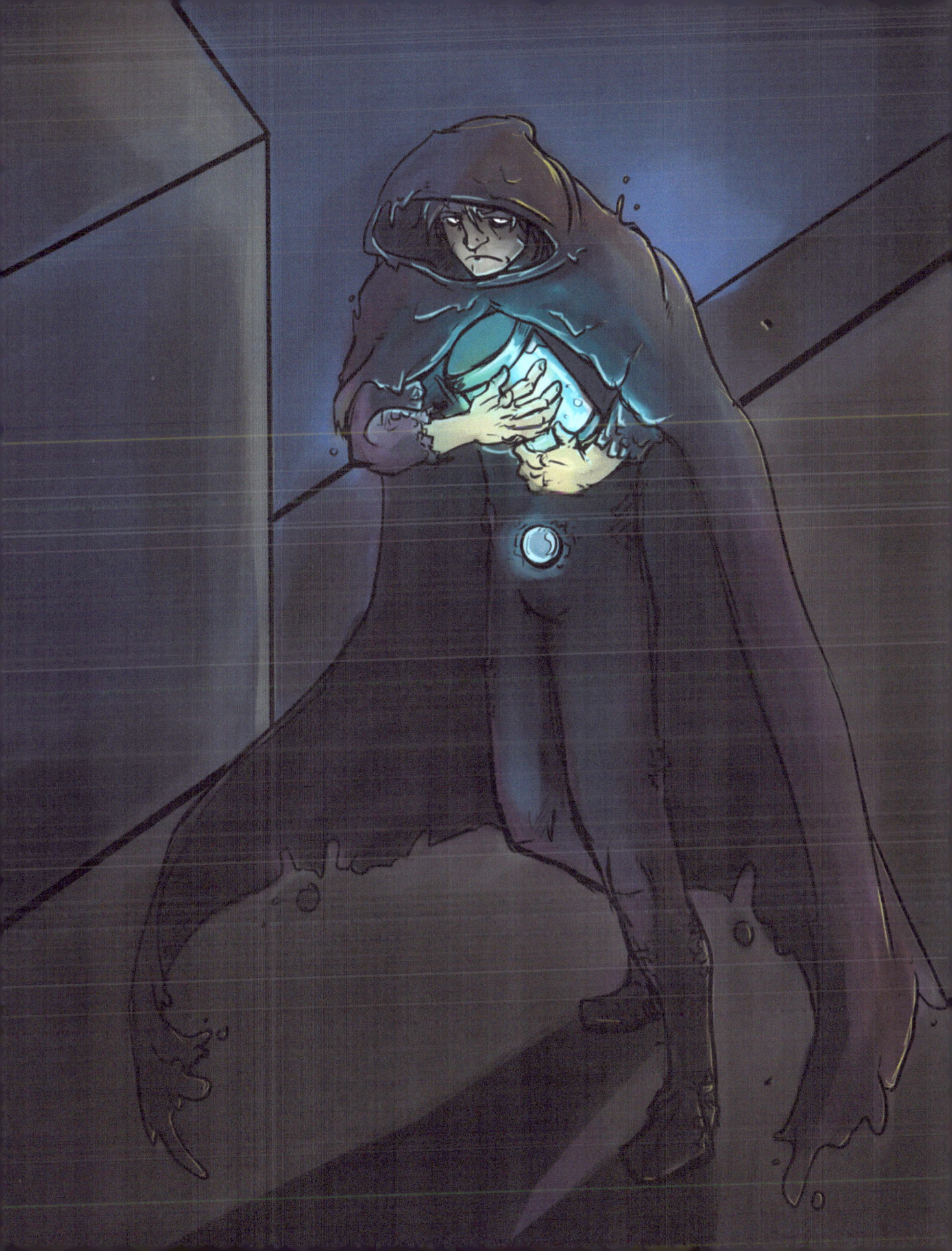

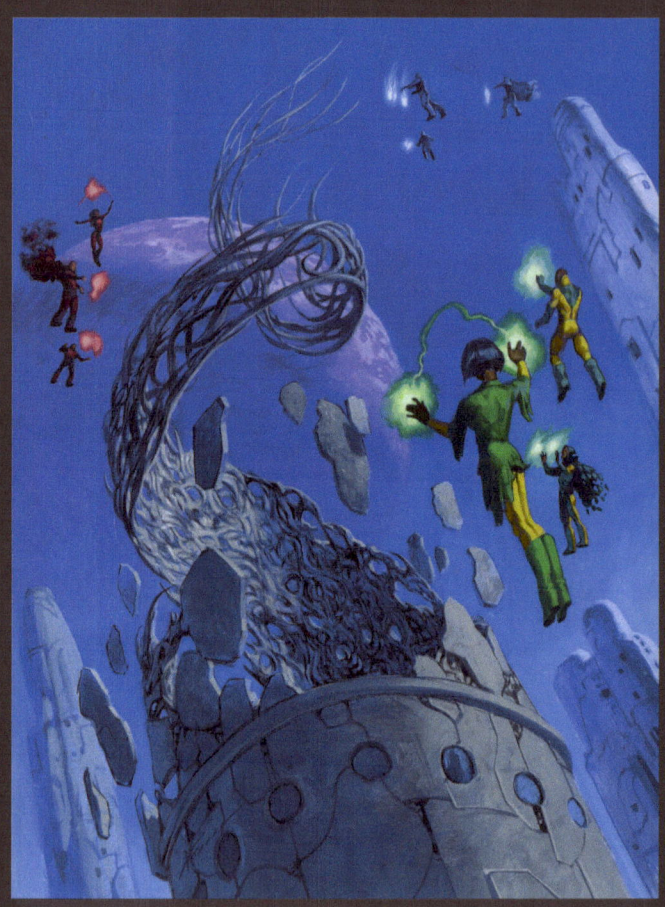

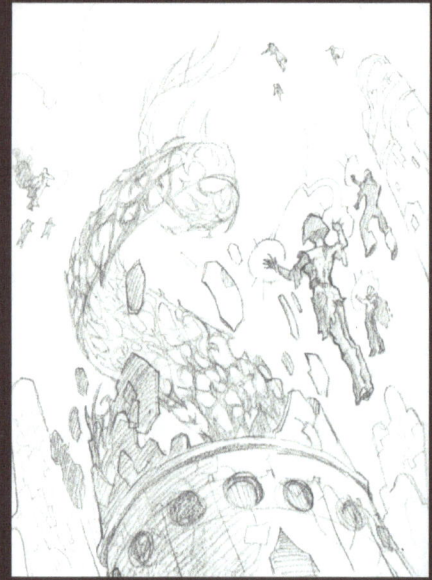

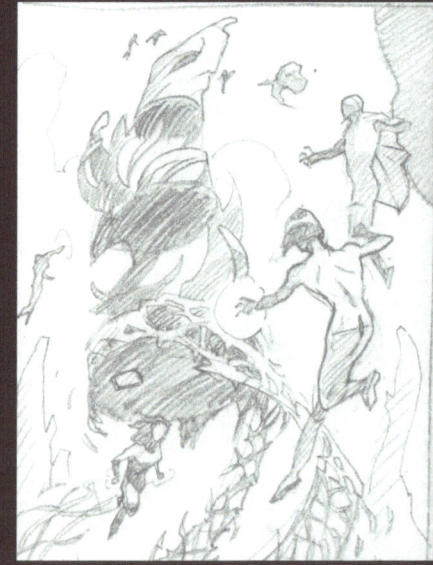

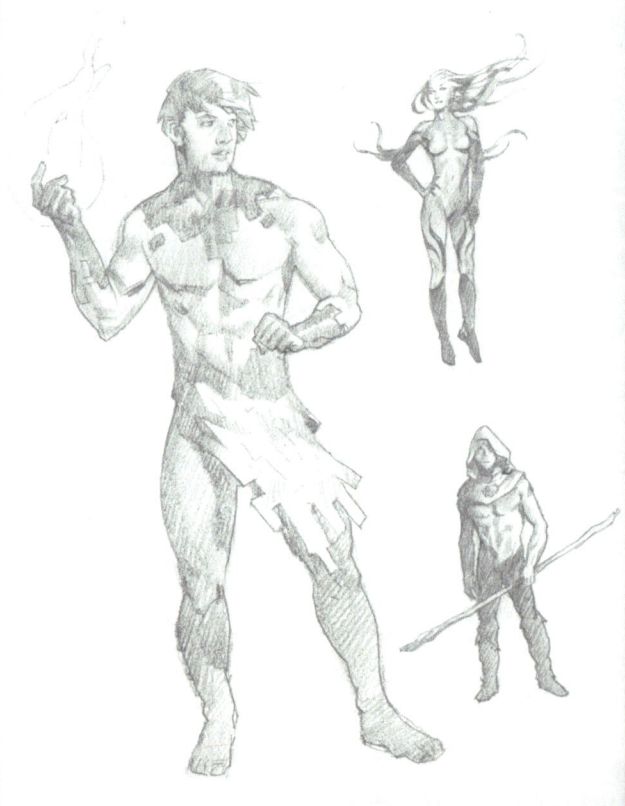

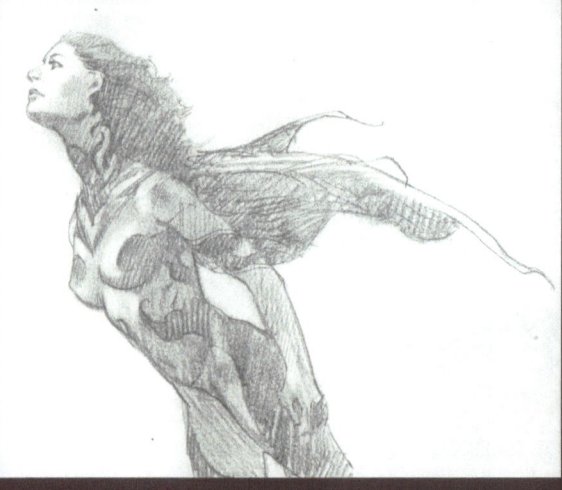

Sketches by Christopher Moeller

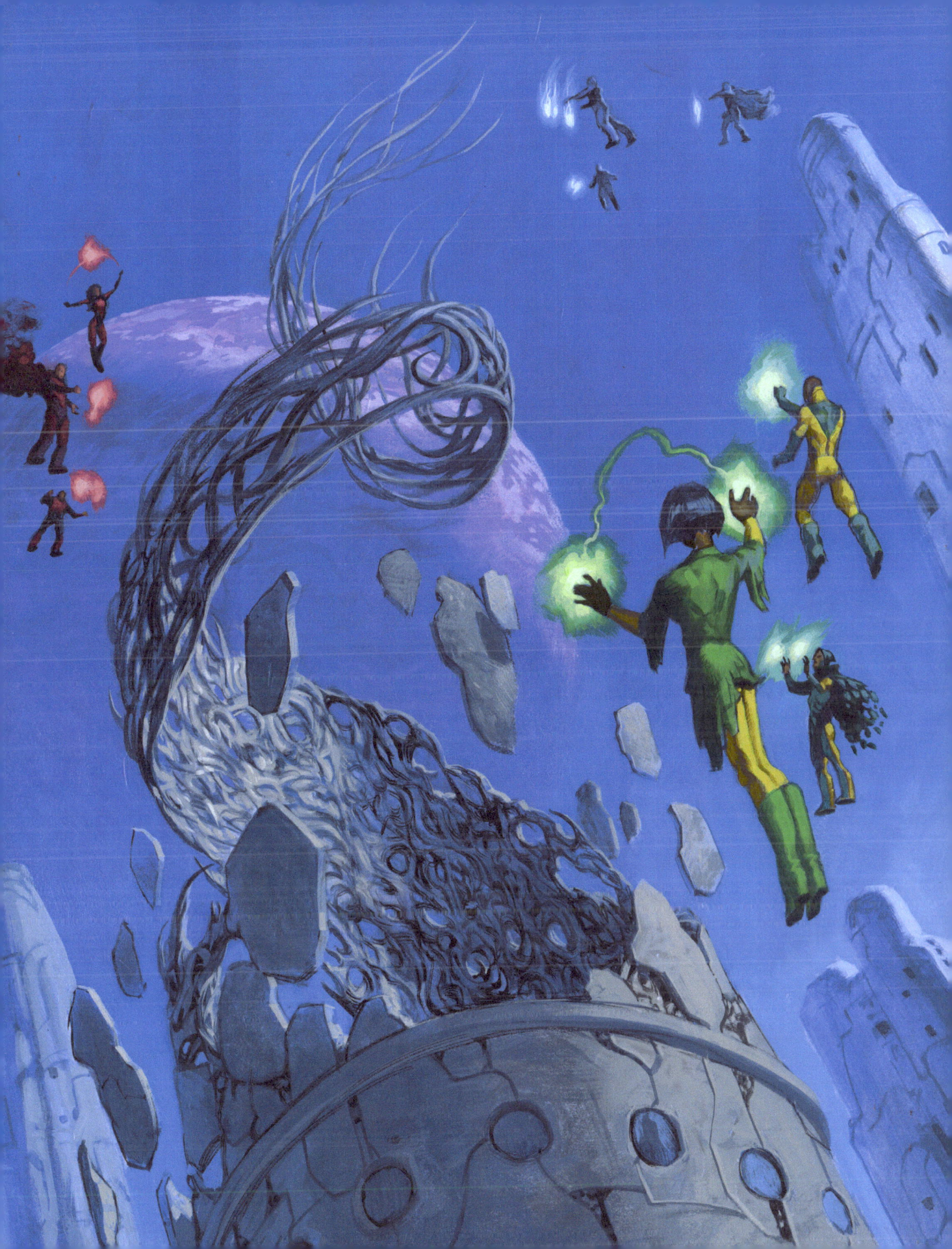

## The Trailer

The images in this section are categorized as "The Trailer" because they were originally created for a marketing video for Imbue - a trailer for the game. I repurposed the illustrations for the book where needed.

It was artist Jason Swope who sparked the idea of a trailer. I was at the beginning of what turned out to be my "writing career" and had no idea how to explain Imbue in a single paragraph (which is kind of important). After expressing my grievances about this to Jason, he was reminded of the opening credits of 80s cartoons. Those cartoons had long introductions that told the background story, like a trailer. And that's when the solution became clear. I knew I could write trailers and so I did. I wrote the paragraph easily enough. And then, I figured, why not actually make a trailer for the Kickstarter campaign?

The voice talent for the trailer is a friend I commissioned, Bethany Warner, who is an exceptional talent. And I commissioned Jason Swope to do nearly all the artwork. I did some of the art pieces myself. I got the music from a royalty free website and edited and produced the trailer.

You can find the trailer on YouTube by searching for "Cryptiquest" or by directly going to:
https://www.youtube.com/watch?v=65bfC5xSgl4

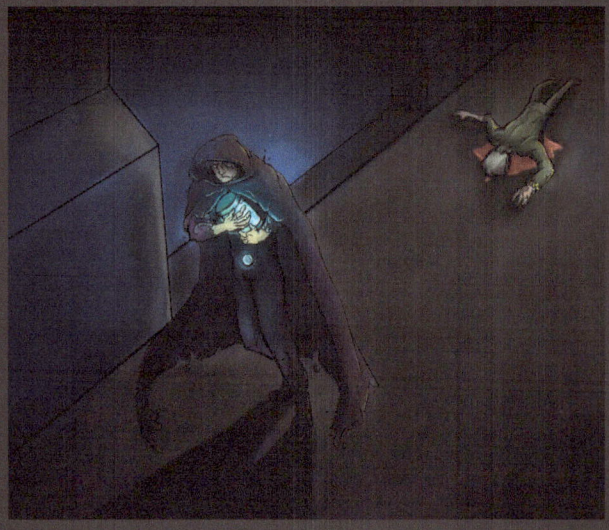

**Artwork by Jason Swope**
This was the piece also used for the Chapter 4 background. I really loved the drip cape and the look on this character's face was perfect for the "Antagonist" theme of the chapter. But there was more to this scene than what was featured in the book.

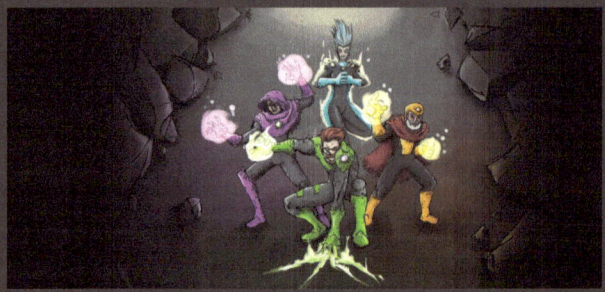

This was a piece that I tried to create and then asked Jason to redo.

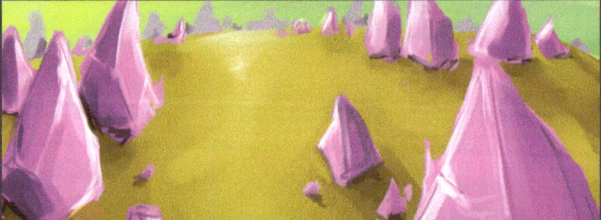

This piece was not included in the book, but I figured I'd show it here since it was in the trailer. I asked Jason for a quick rendering of a weird planet and this fit the bill.

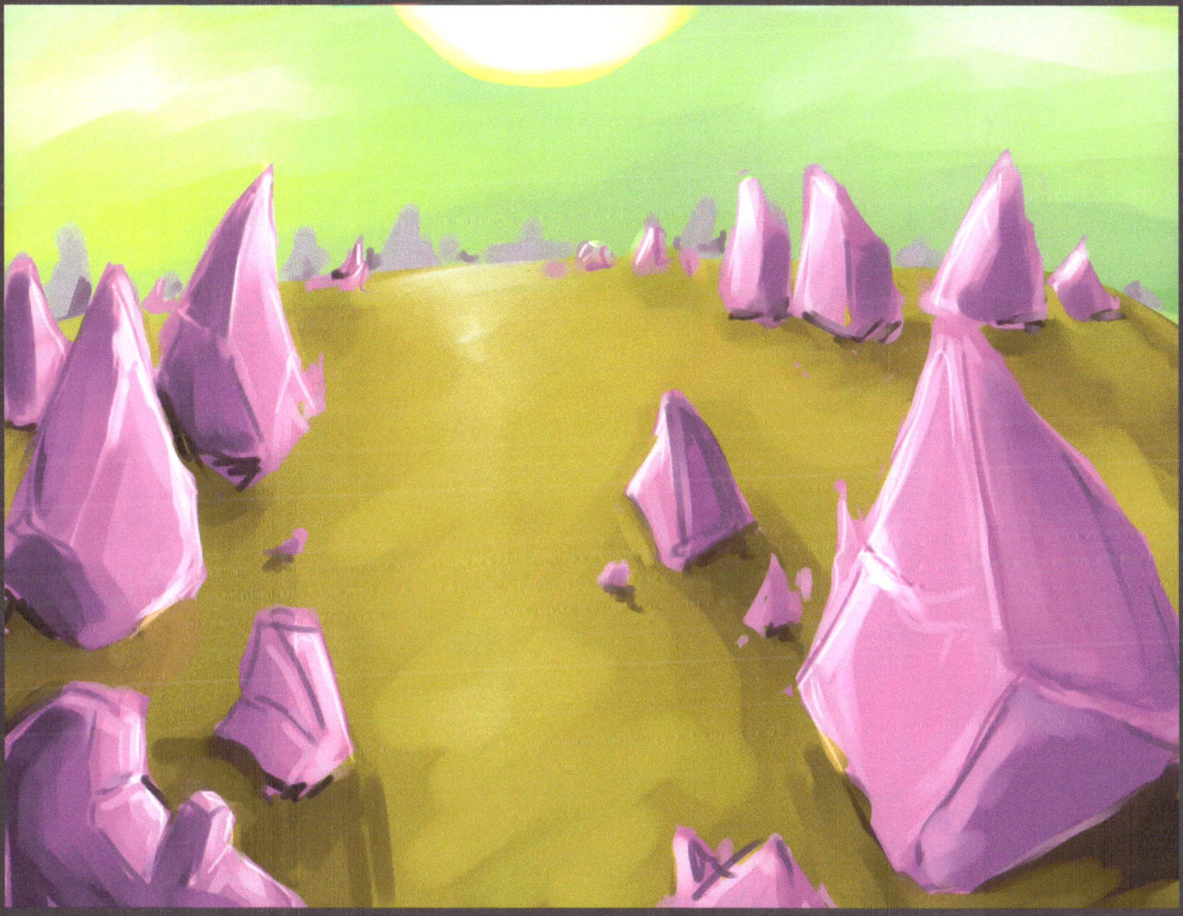

19

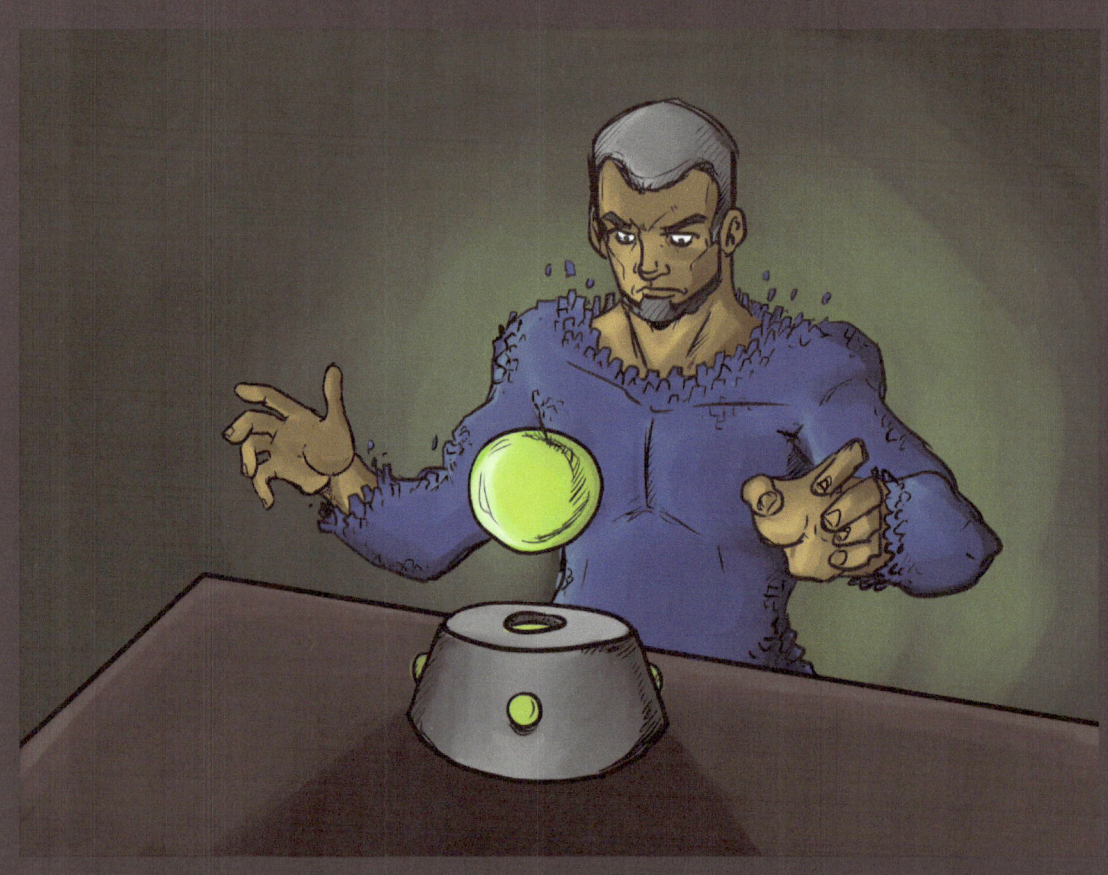

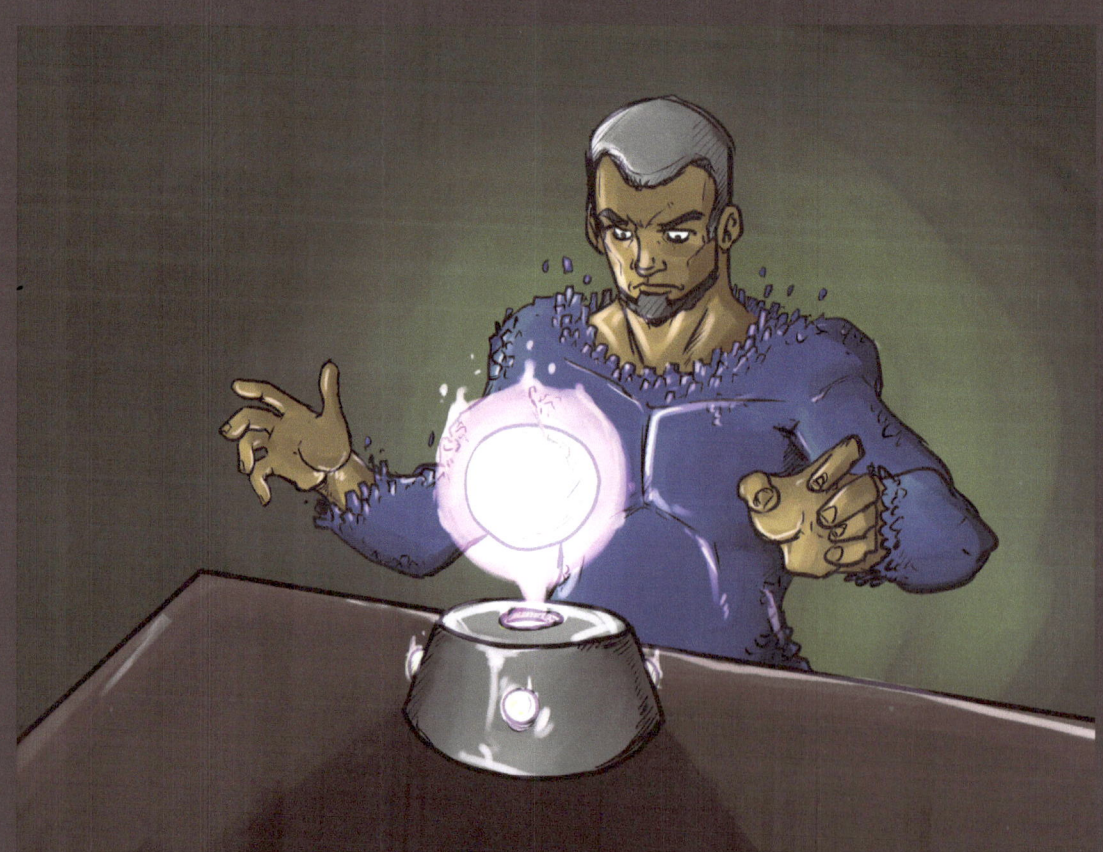

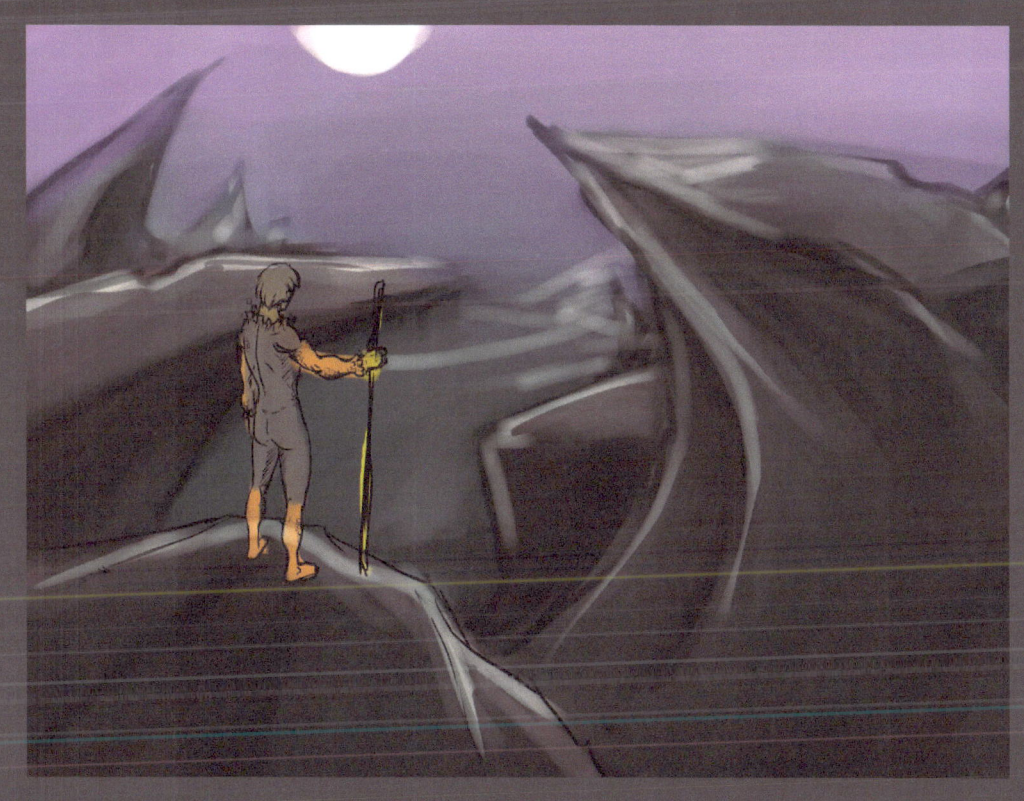

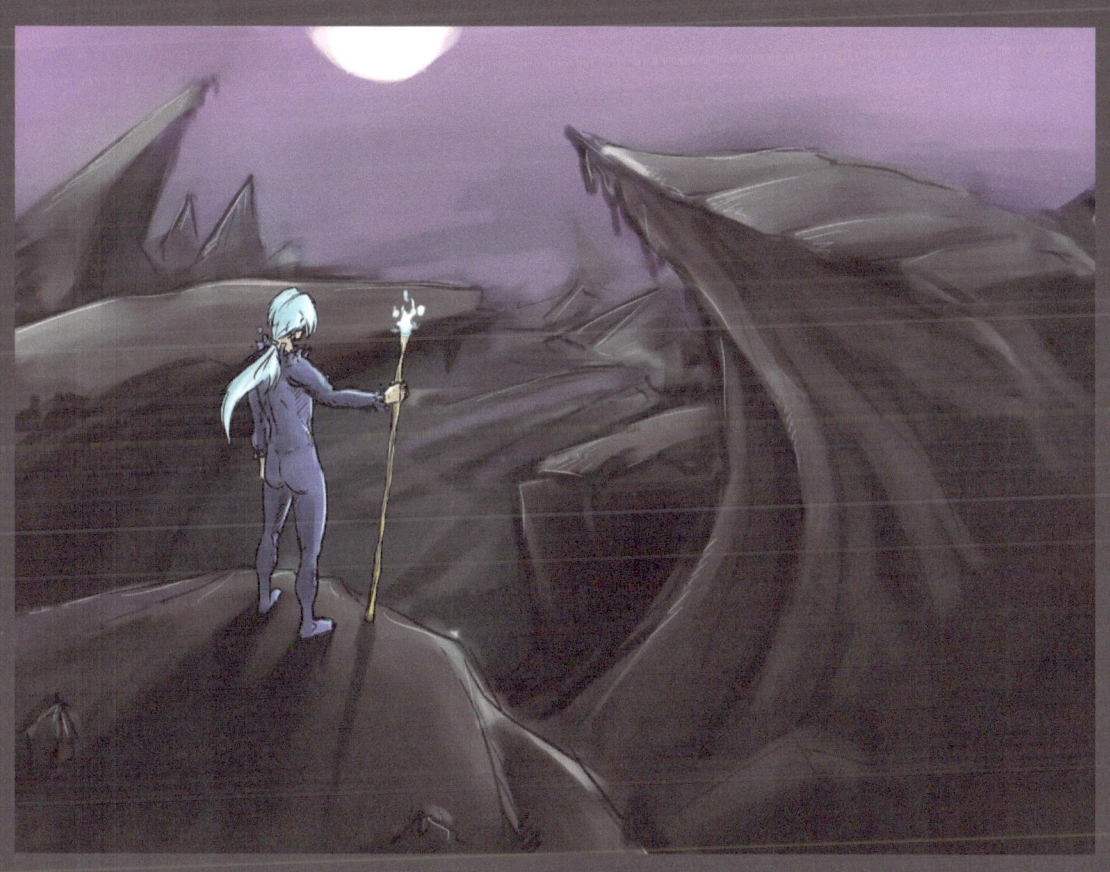

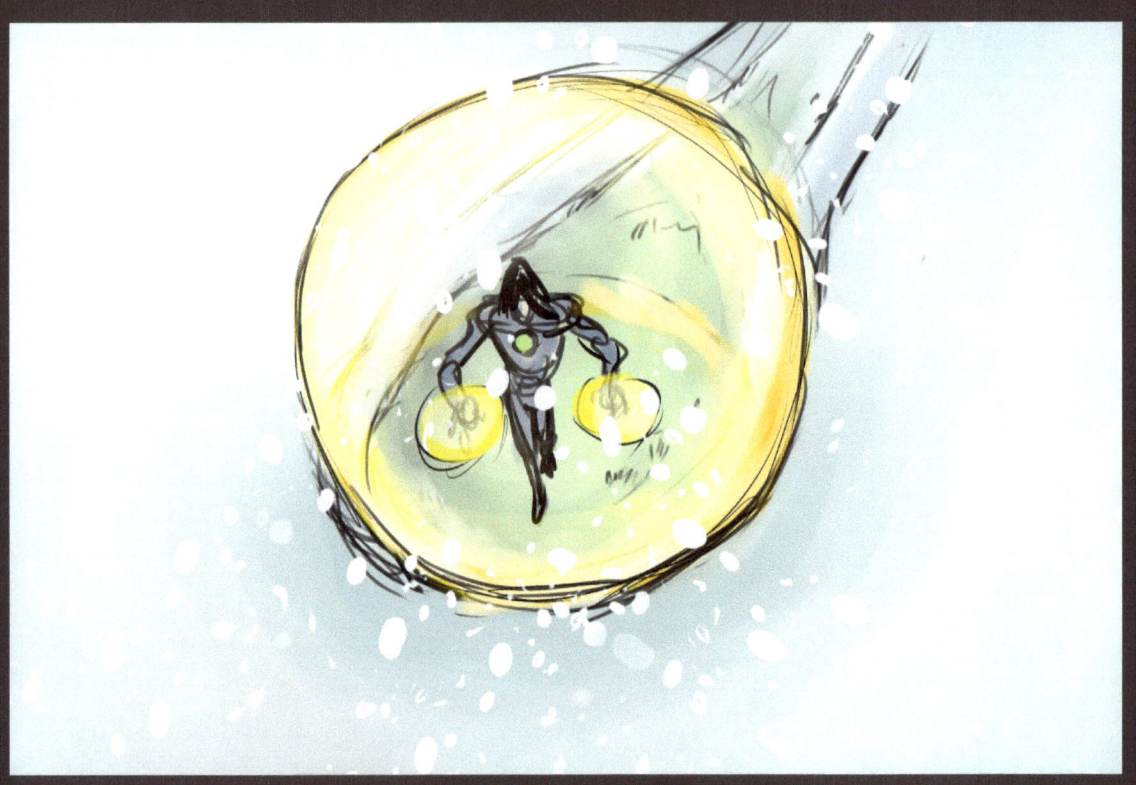

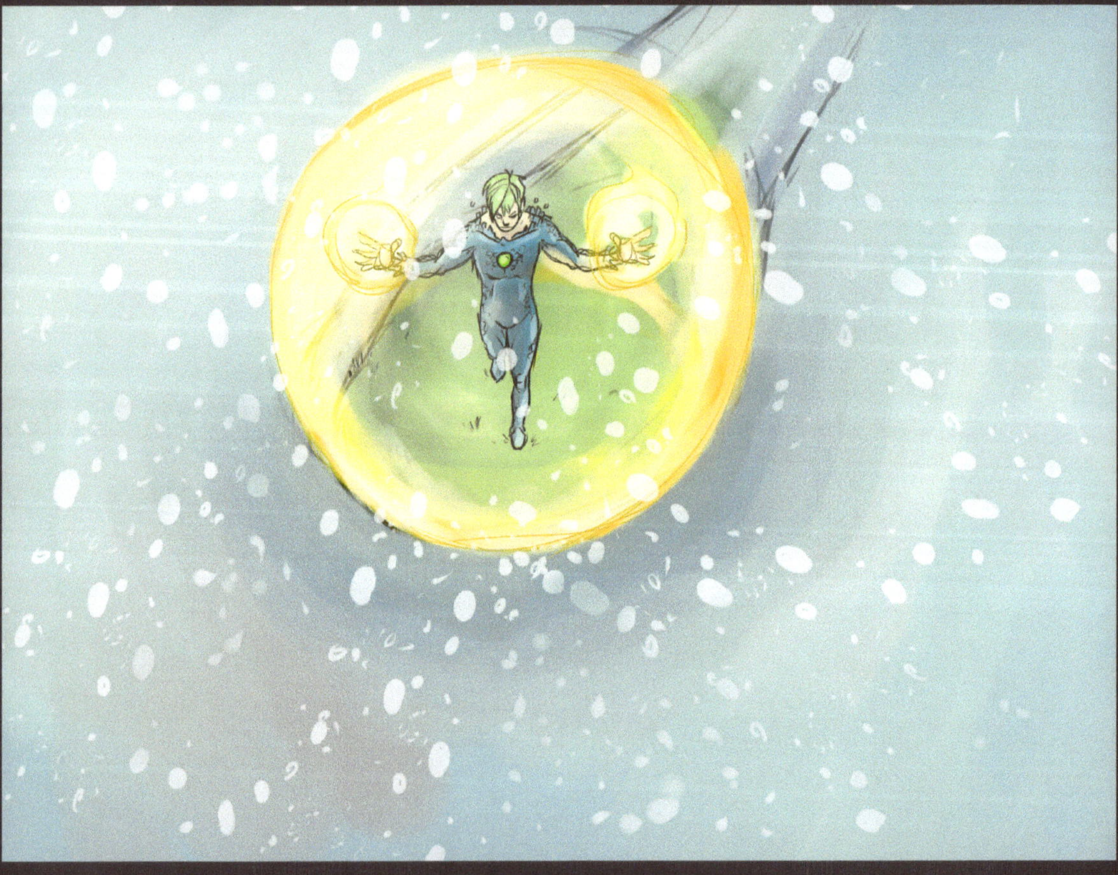

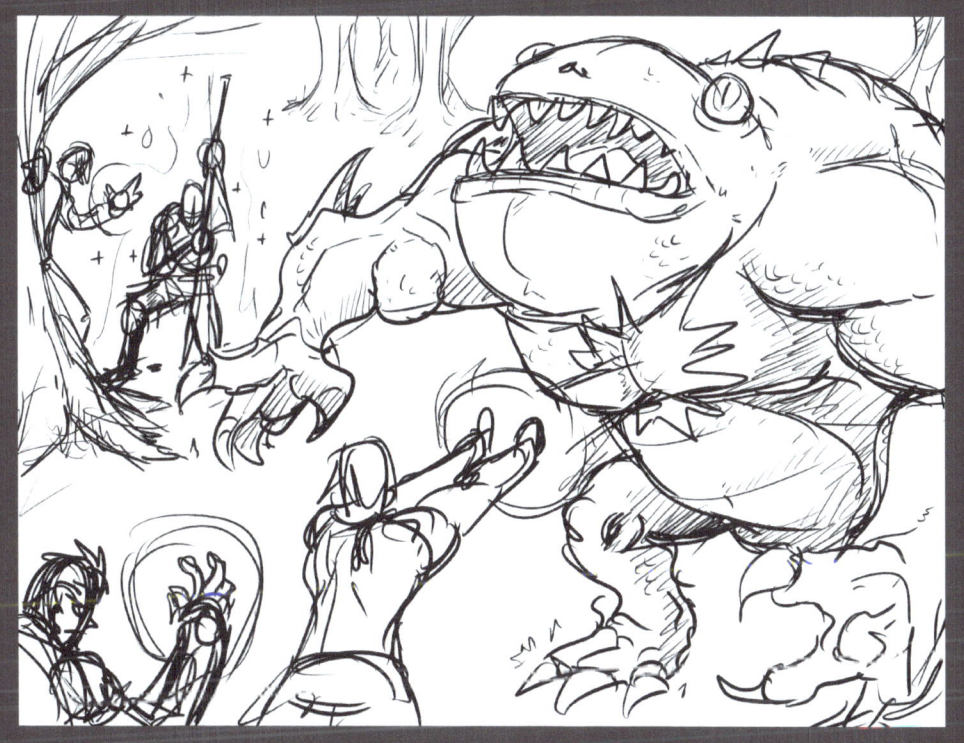

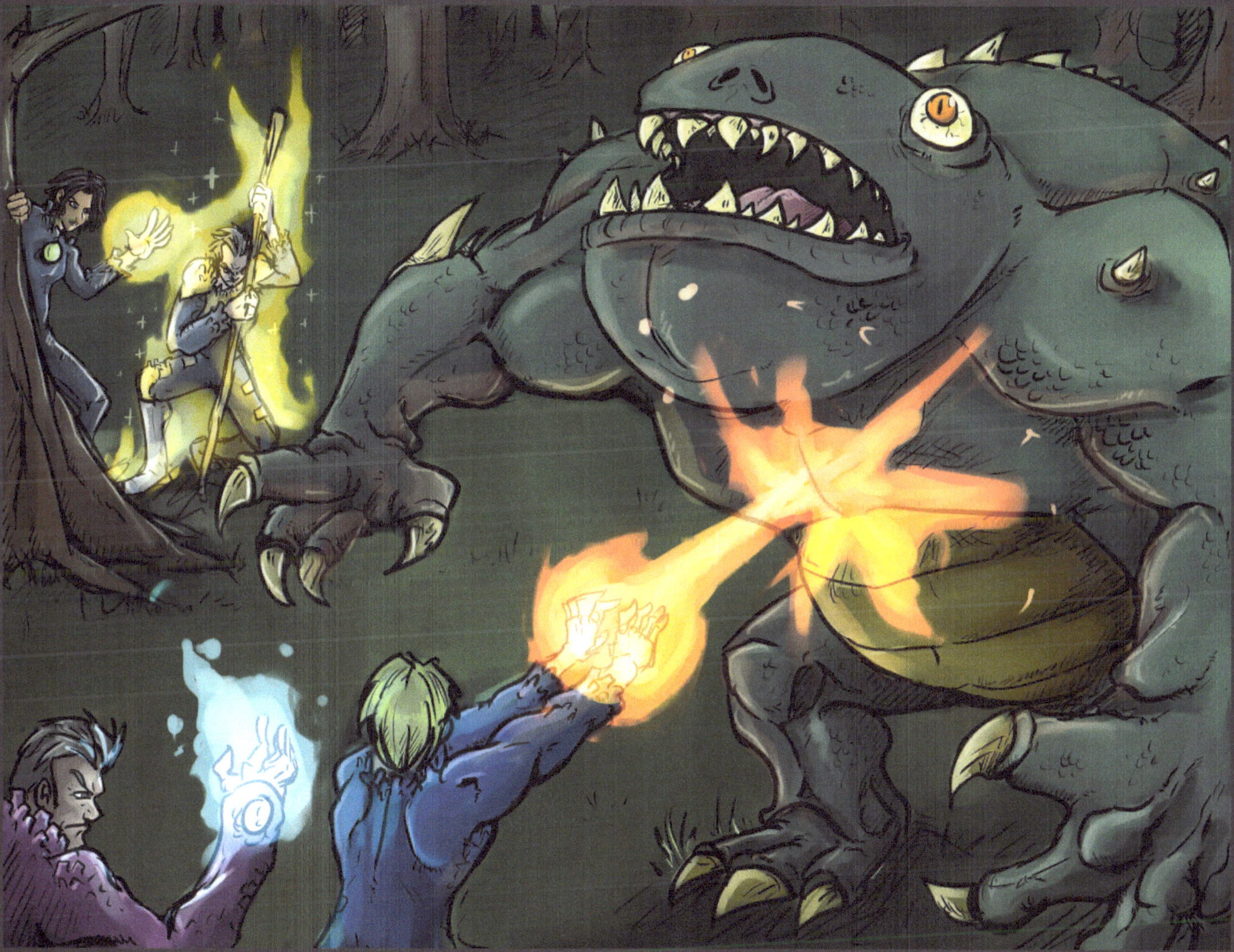

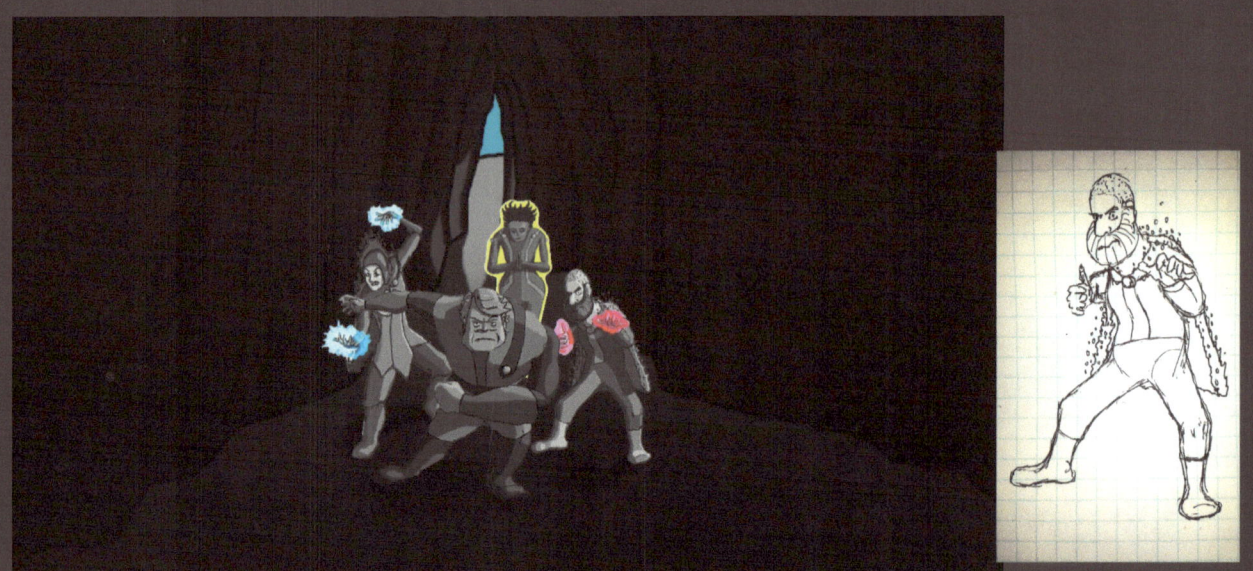

References made by Luke Reynolds

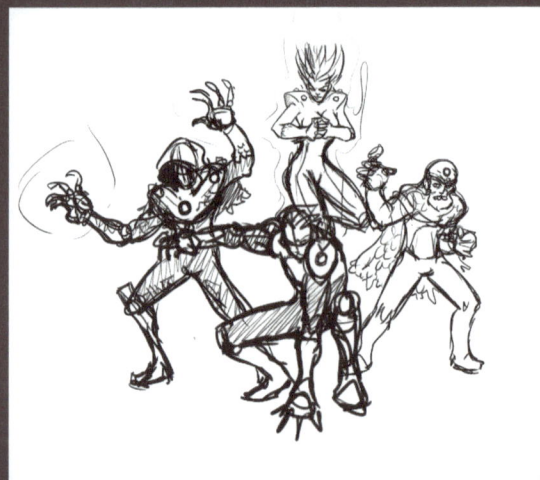

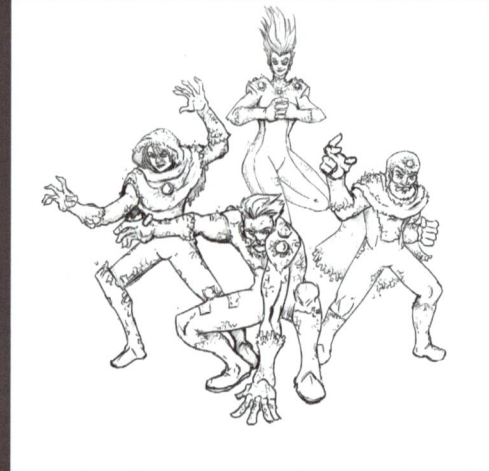

Sketcthes by Jason Swope

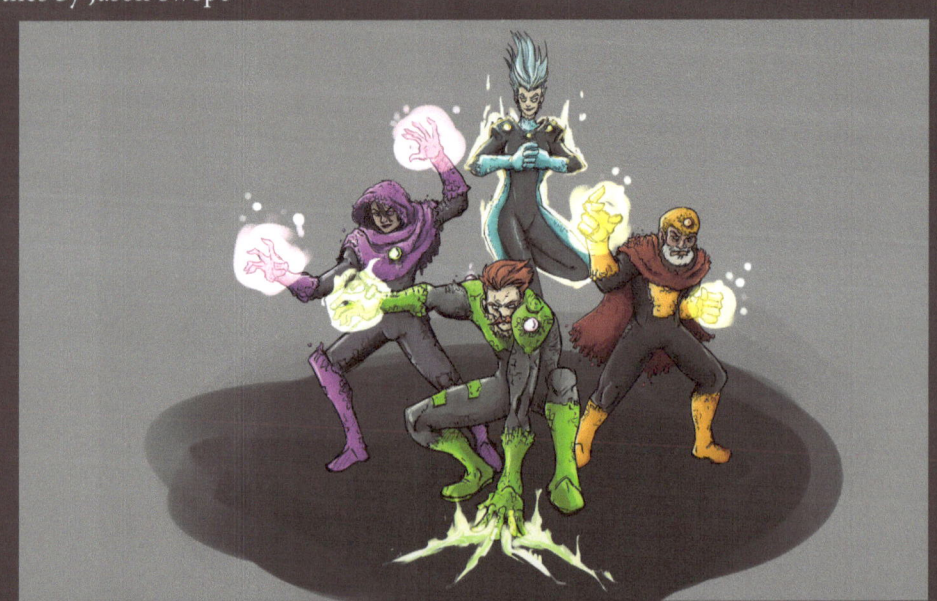

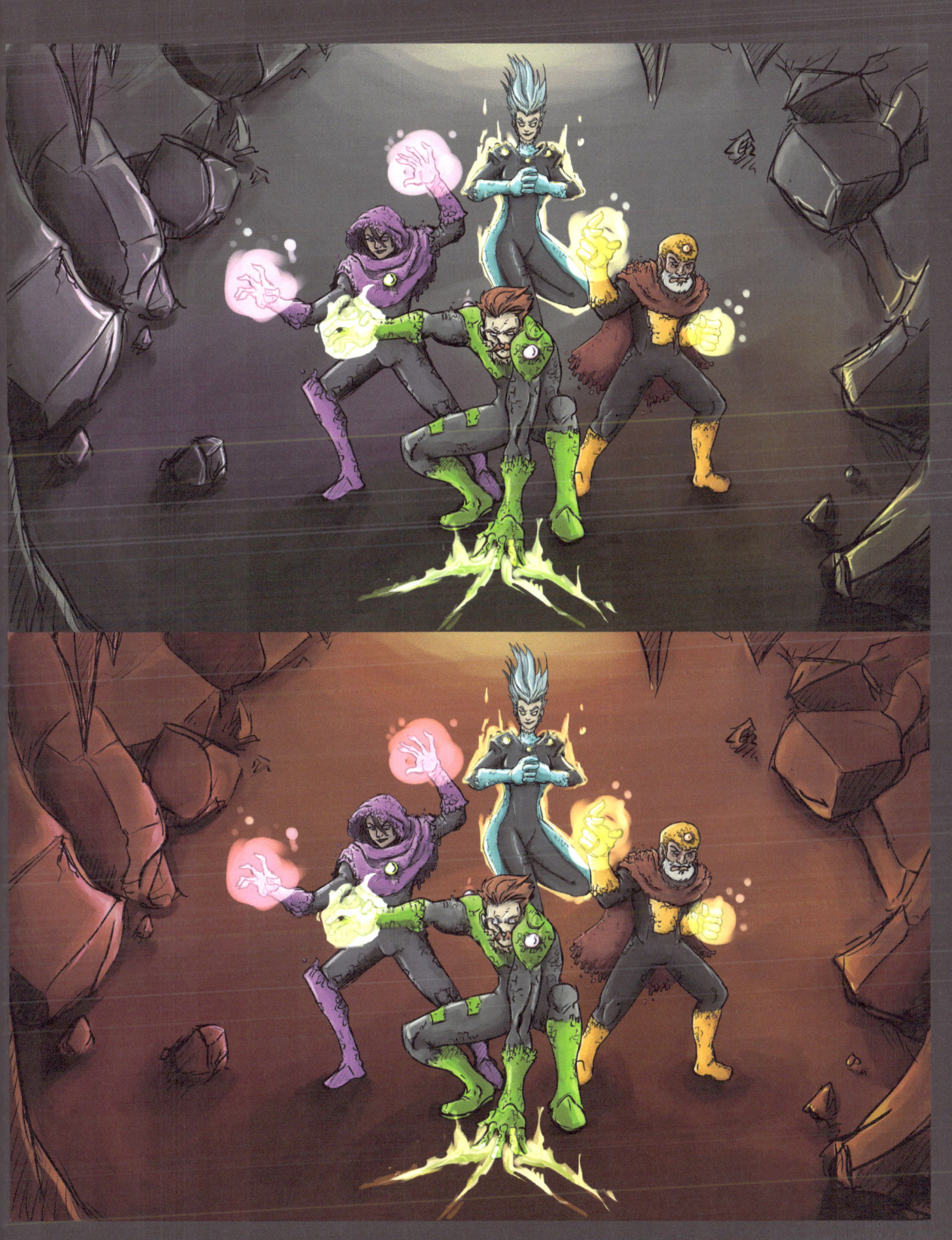

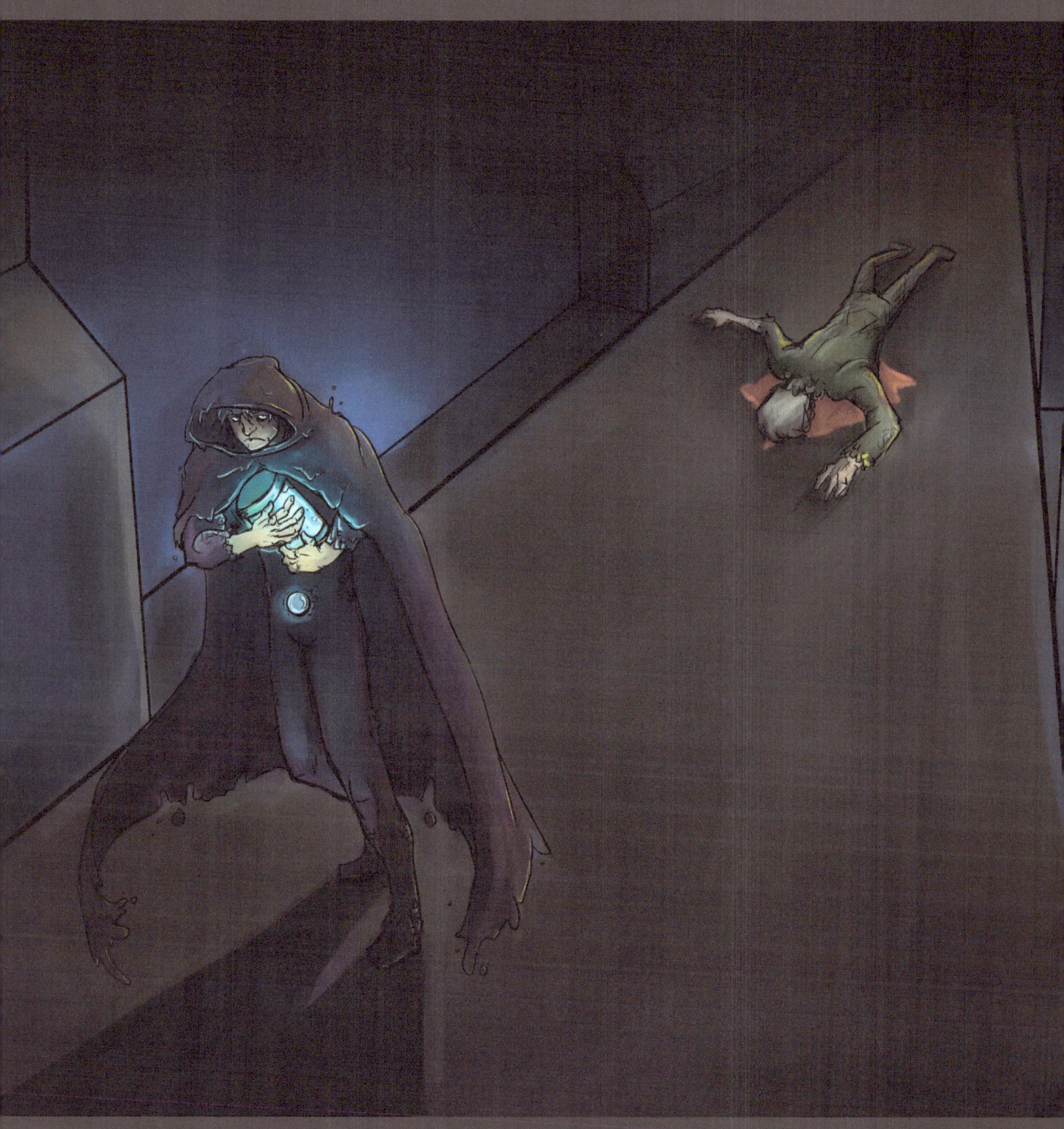

**Artwork by Luke Reynolds**

An example of artwork that I do in a pinch. I was toying around with buildings. I didn't want structures to look like blocky skyscrapers or like they were made from Earth building materials. I figured architects would take shapes from nature as inspiration. From the inside, the walls could be transparent - like a two-way mirror, so no need for windows. And structures of upper class would hover in the air.

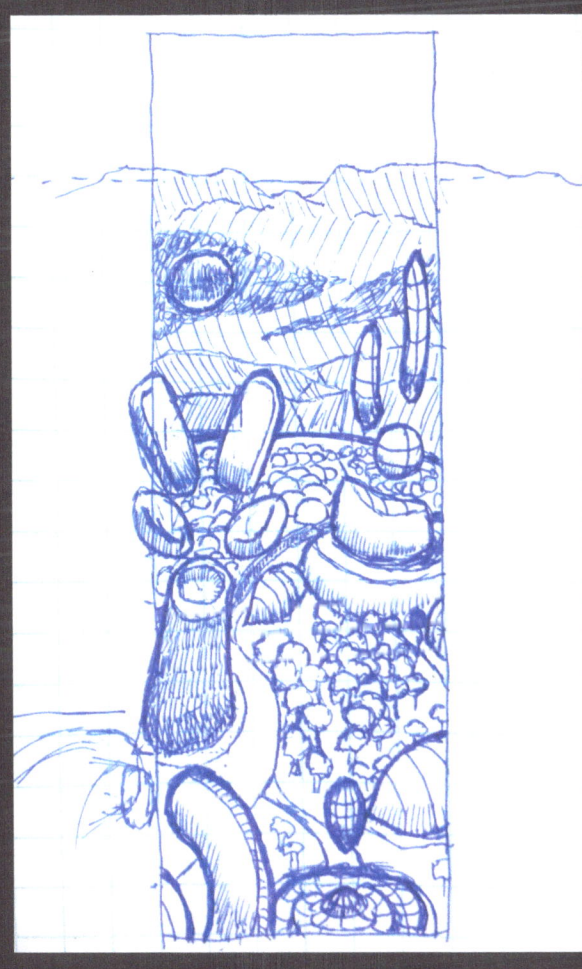

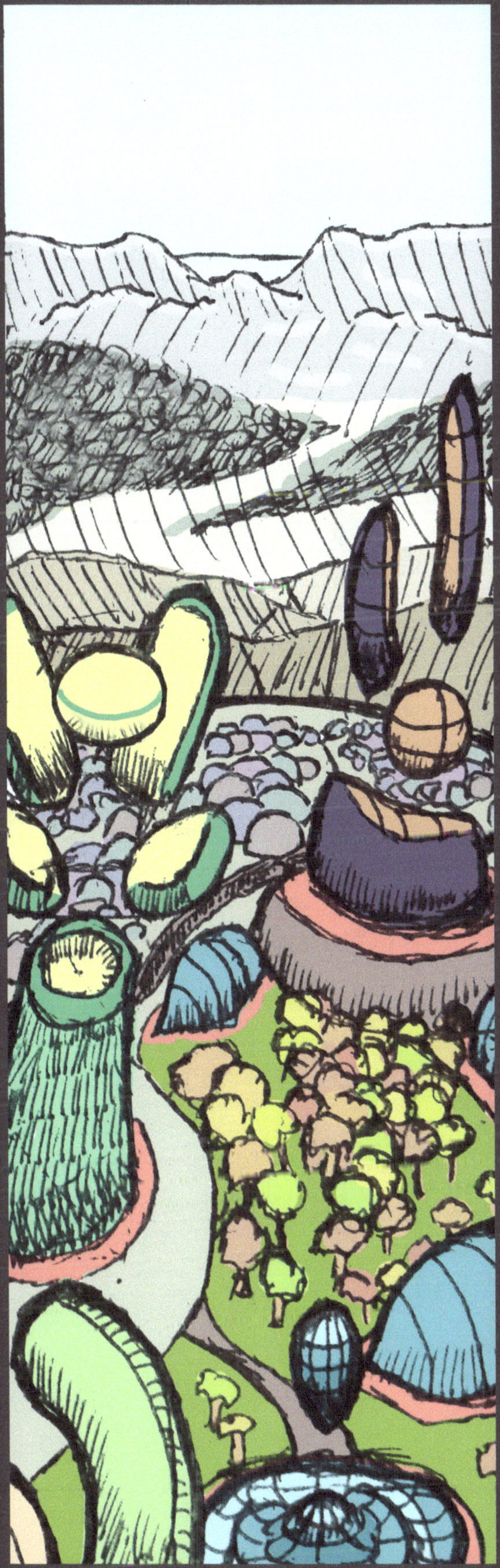

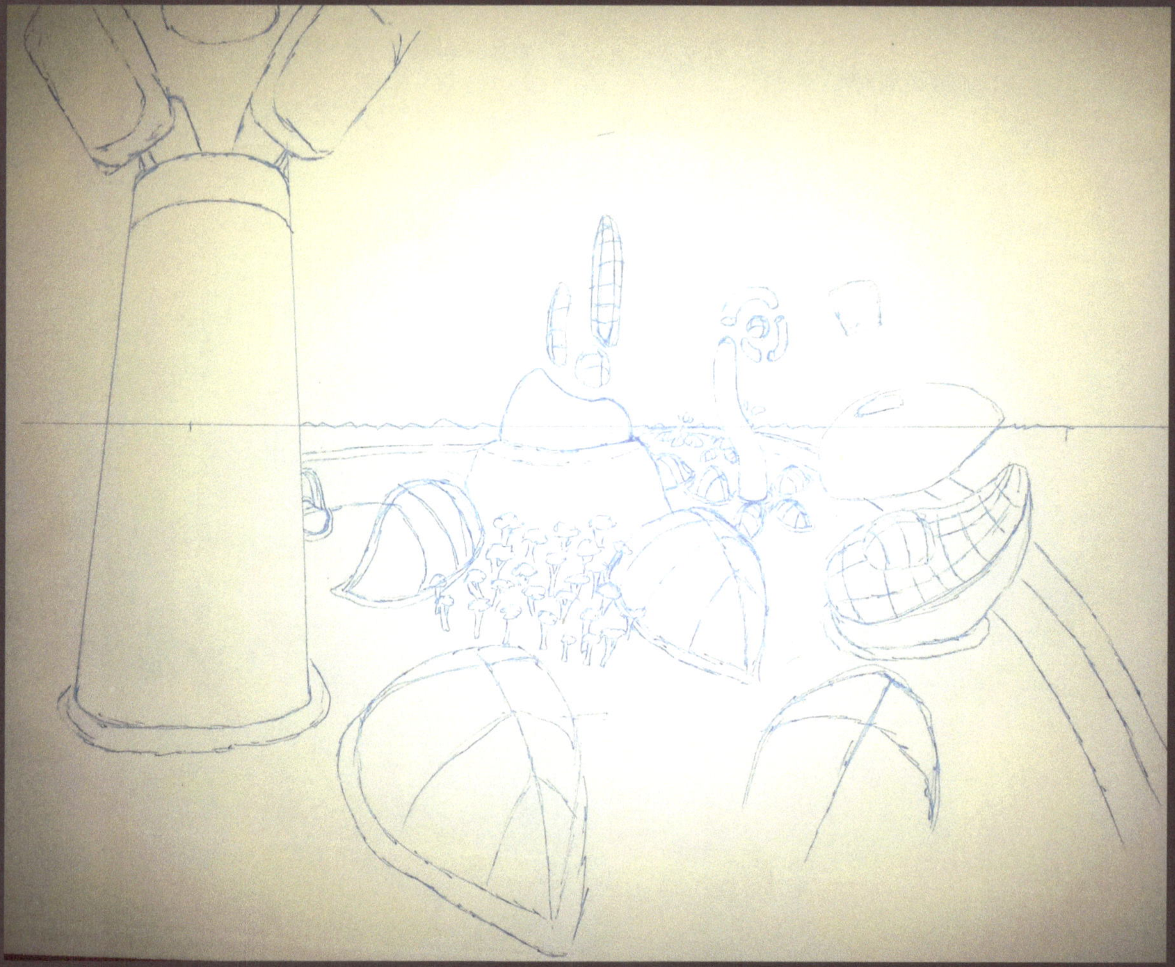

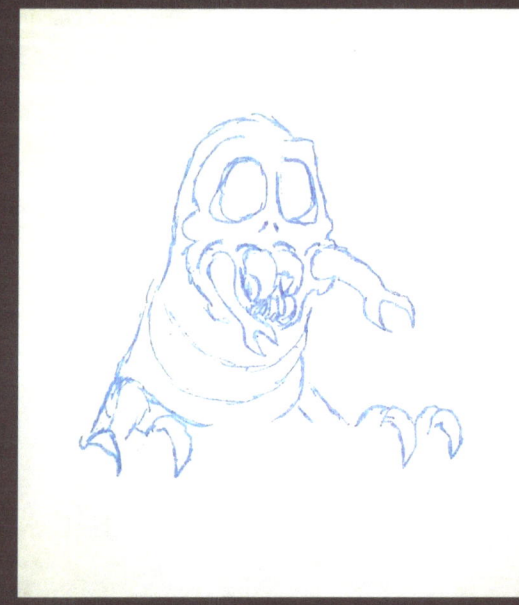

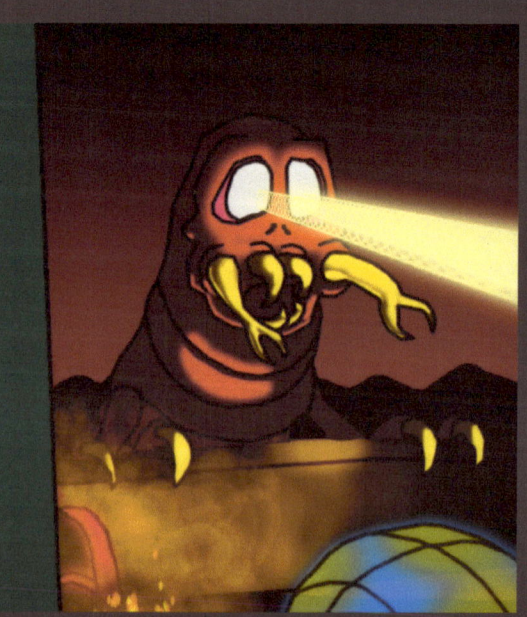

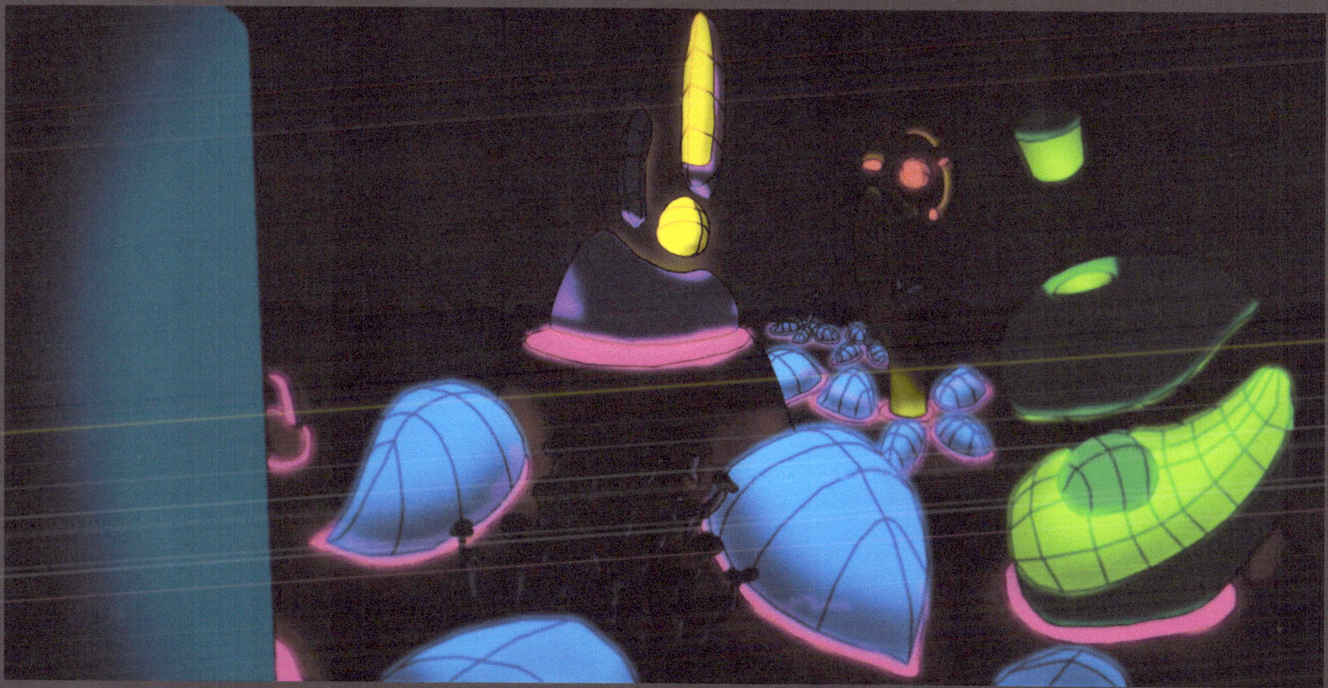

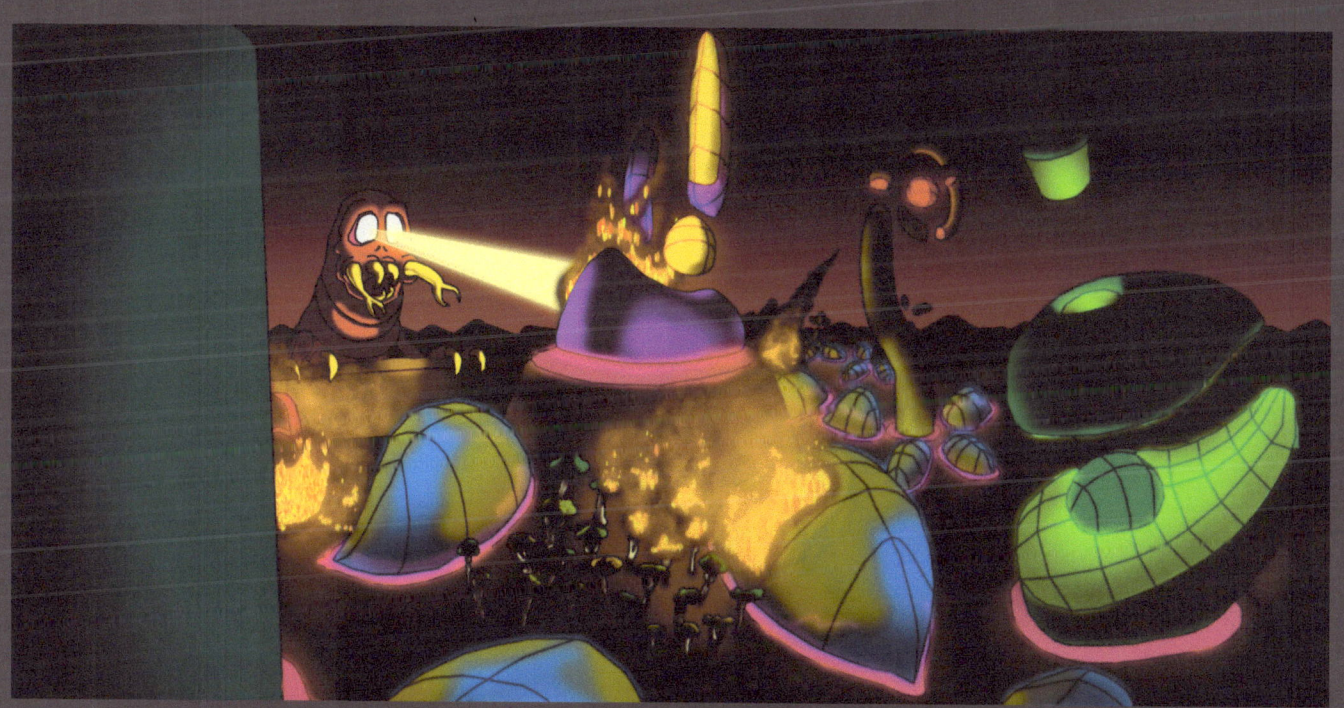

# Supporting Artwork

## Maps by Luke Reynolds

I created these maps digitally. I had fun making them though I would have preferred to commission an illustrator to create these. I plan on doing so for the next edition of Imbue.

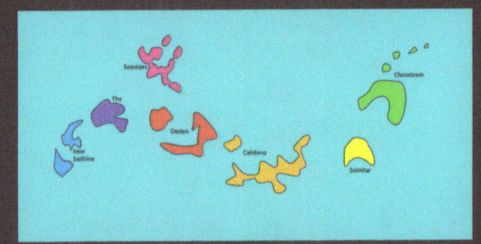

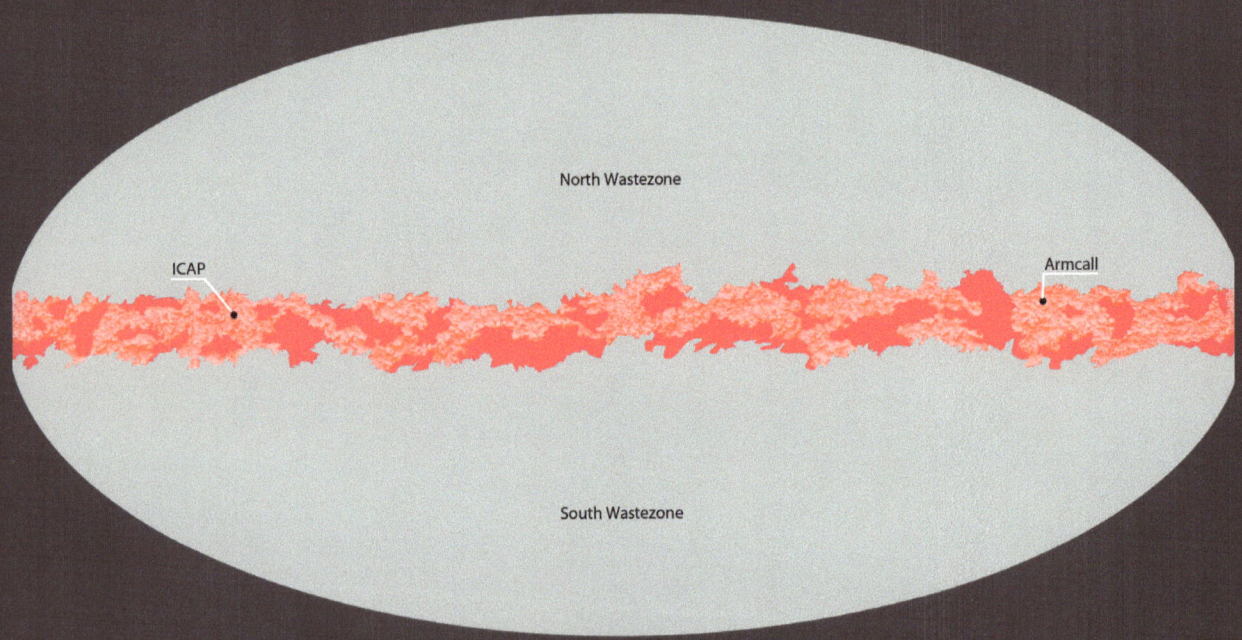

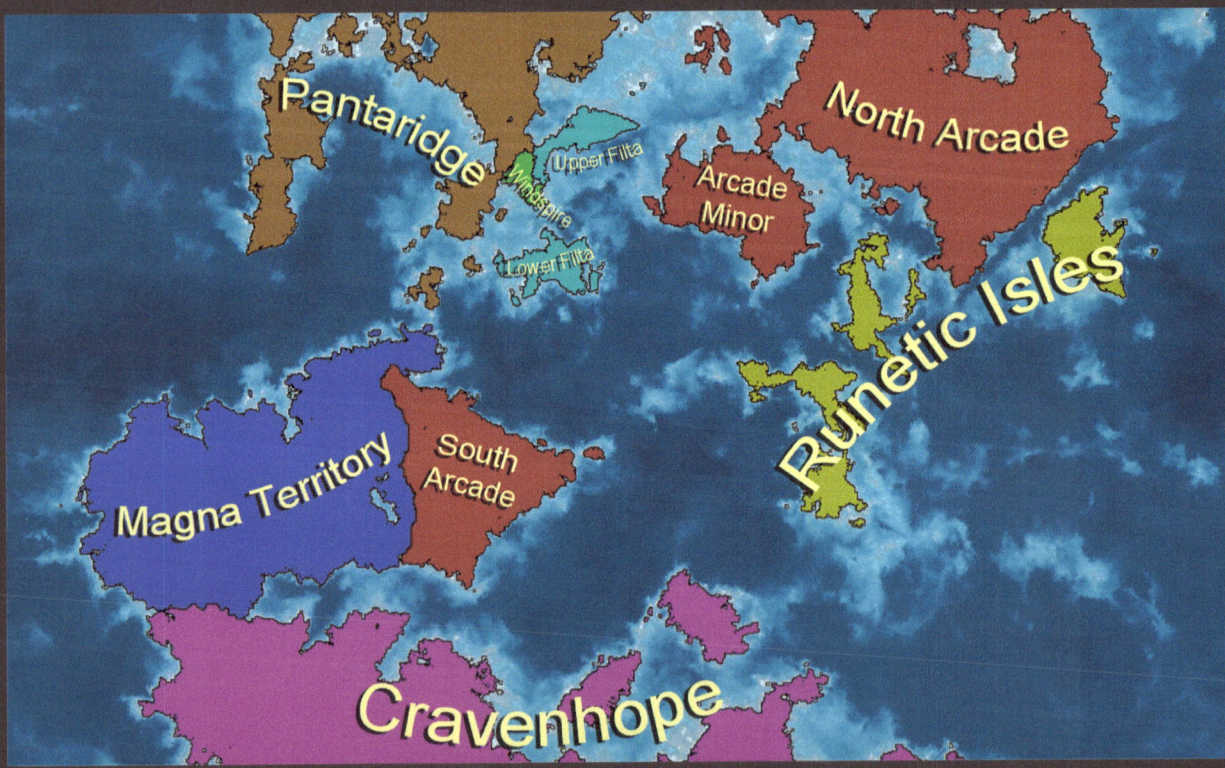

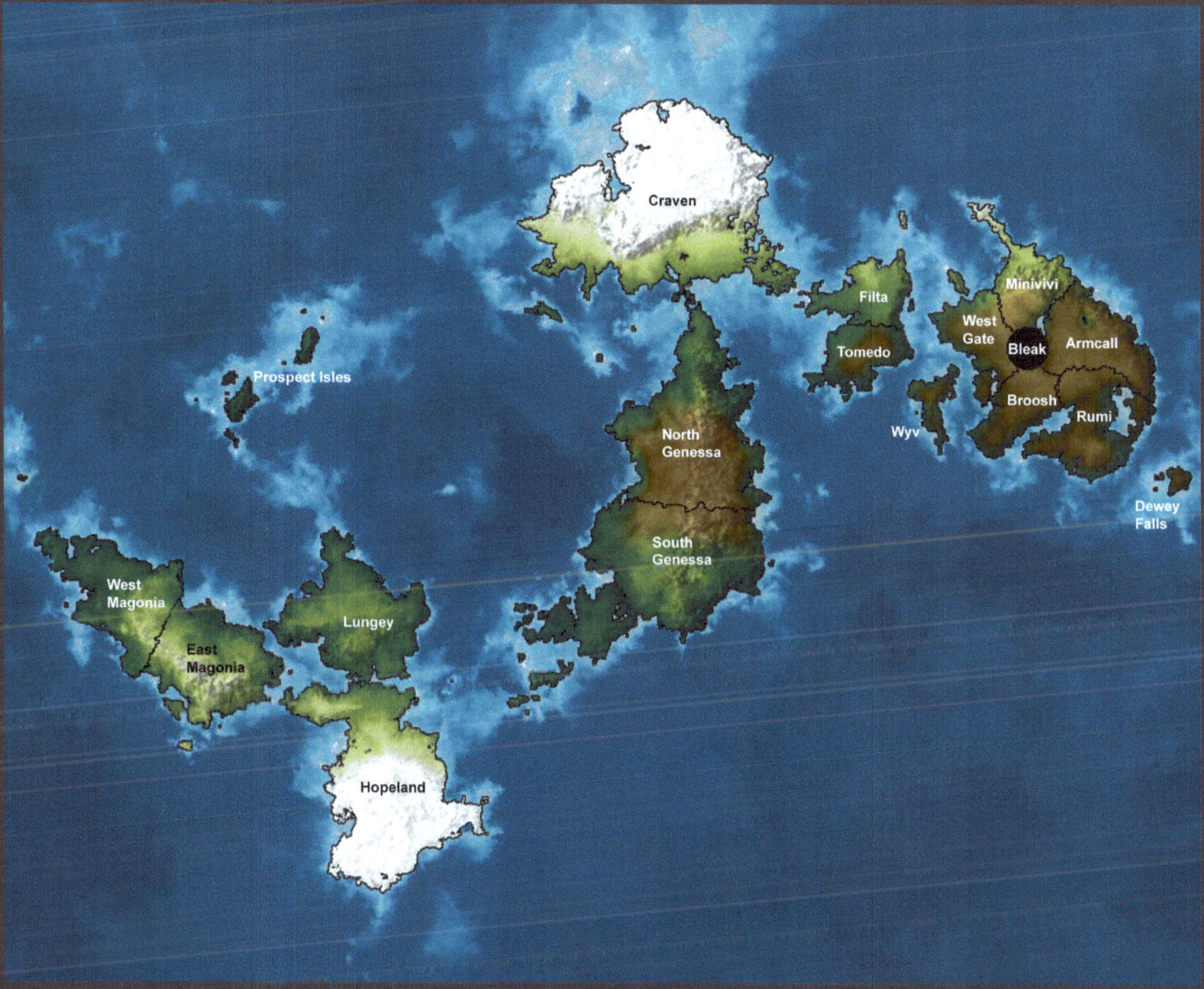

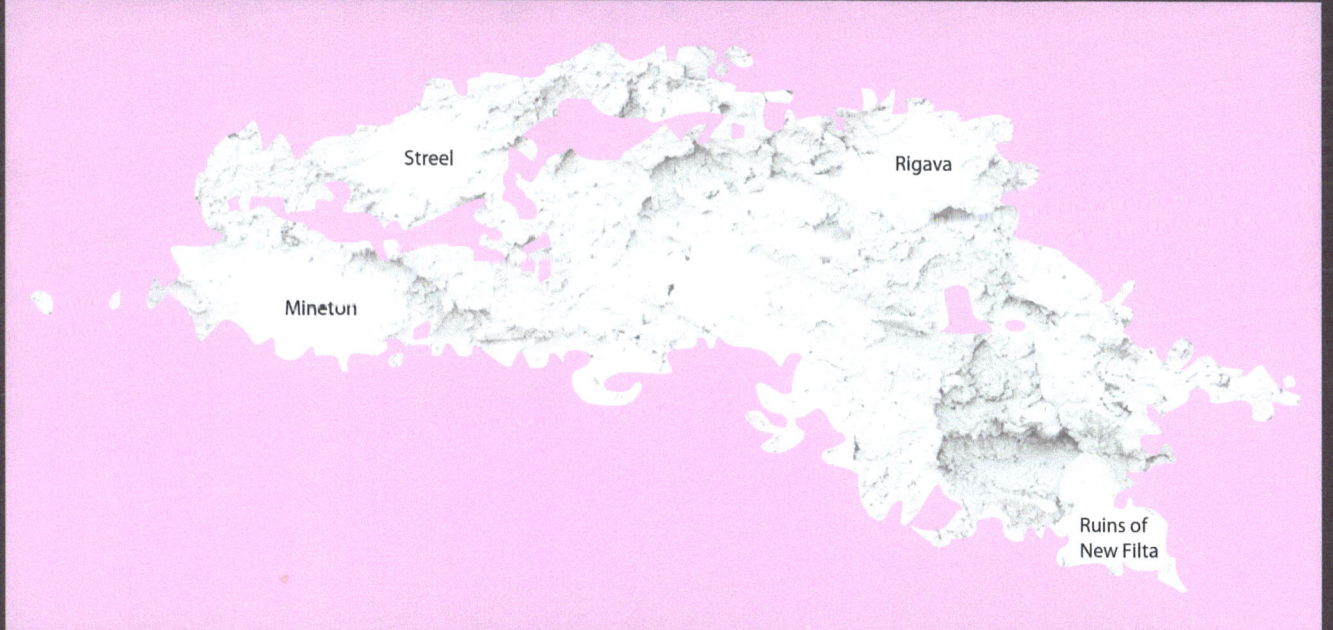

Craven

Filta

Minivivi

West
Gate

Bleak

Armcall

Tomedo

Broosh

Rumi

Prospect Isles

North
Genessa

Wyv

Dewey
Falls

South
Genessa

West
Magonia

Lungey

East
Magonia

Hopeland

Streel

Rigava

Mineton

Ruins of
New Filta

**Antagonist Mugshots by Jason Swope**
I wanted to end this book with these last images because they were so much fun to produce. I commissioned Jason Swope to illustrate four portraits of antagonists. I gave him a summary of each one and the results were perfect. I had a blast incorporating them into the layout.

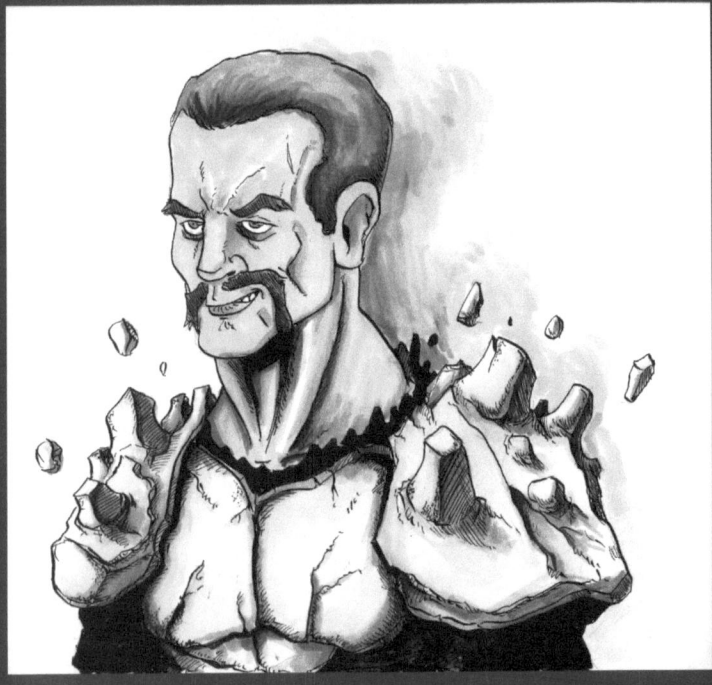

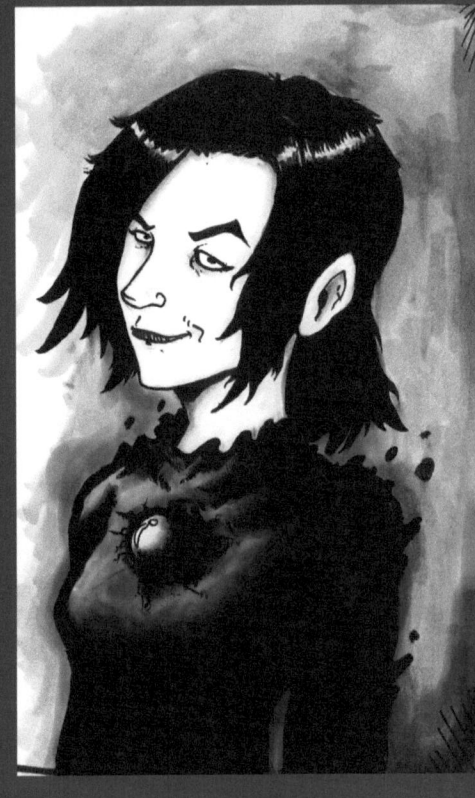

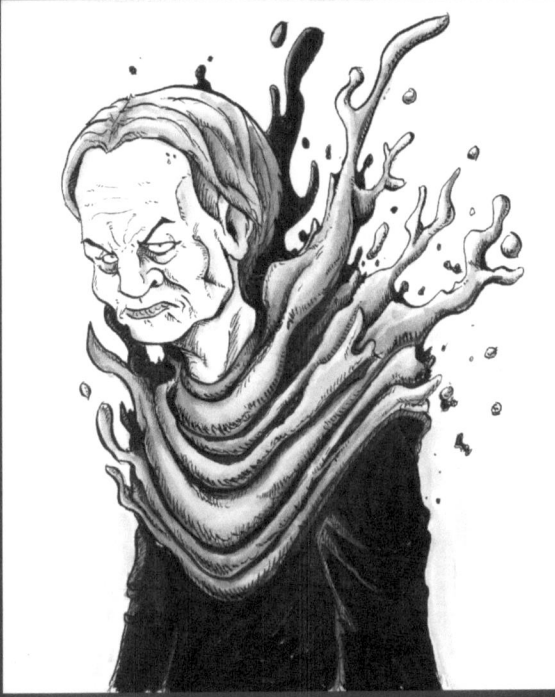

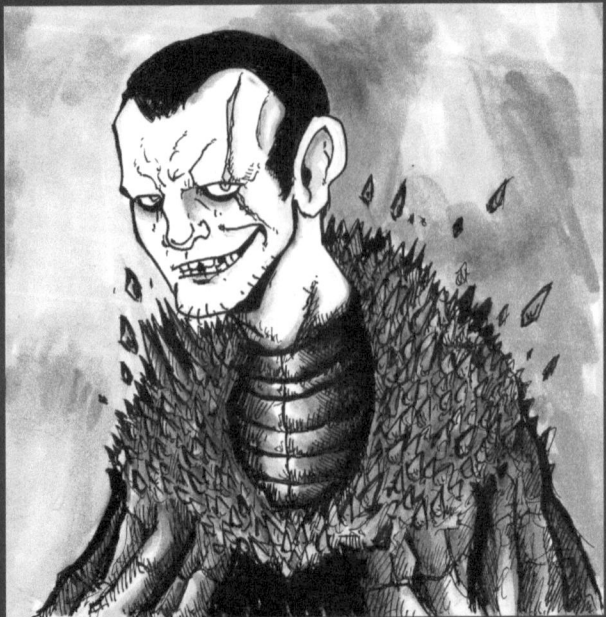

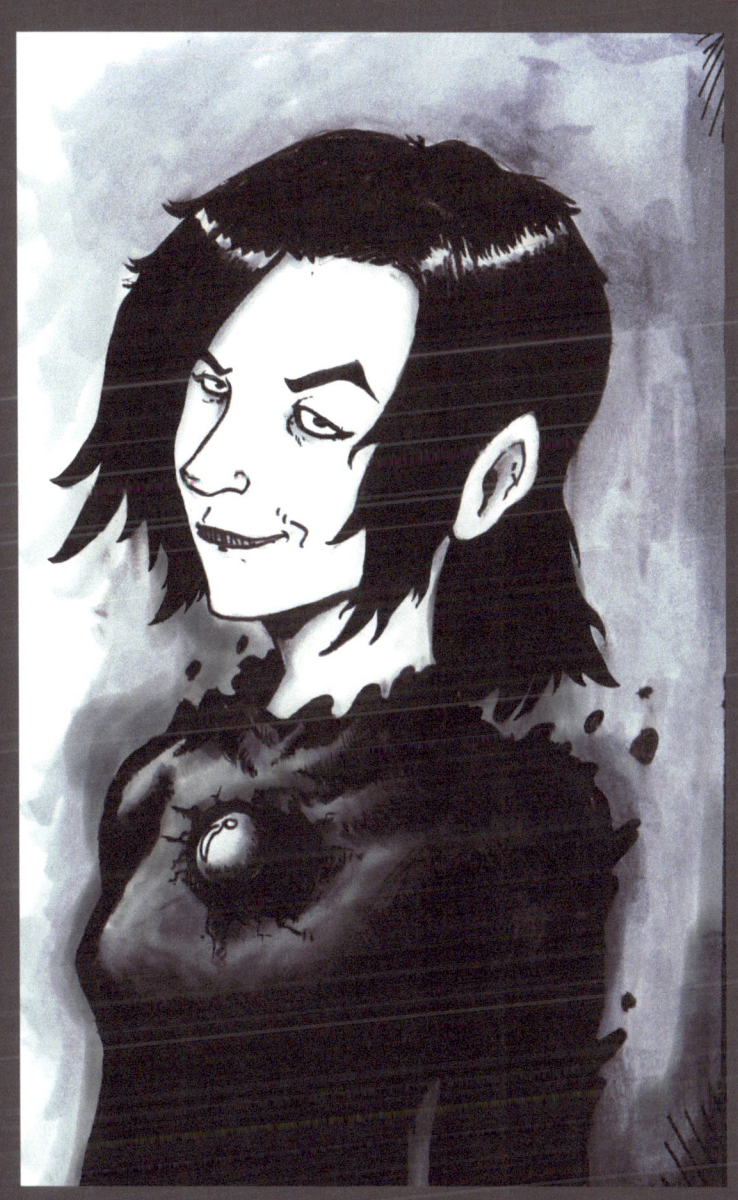

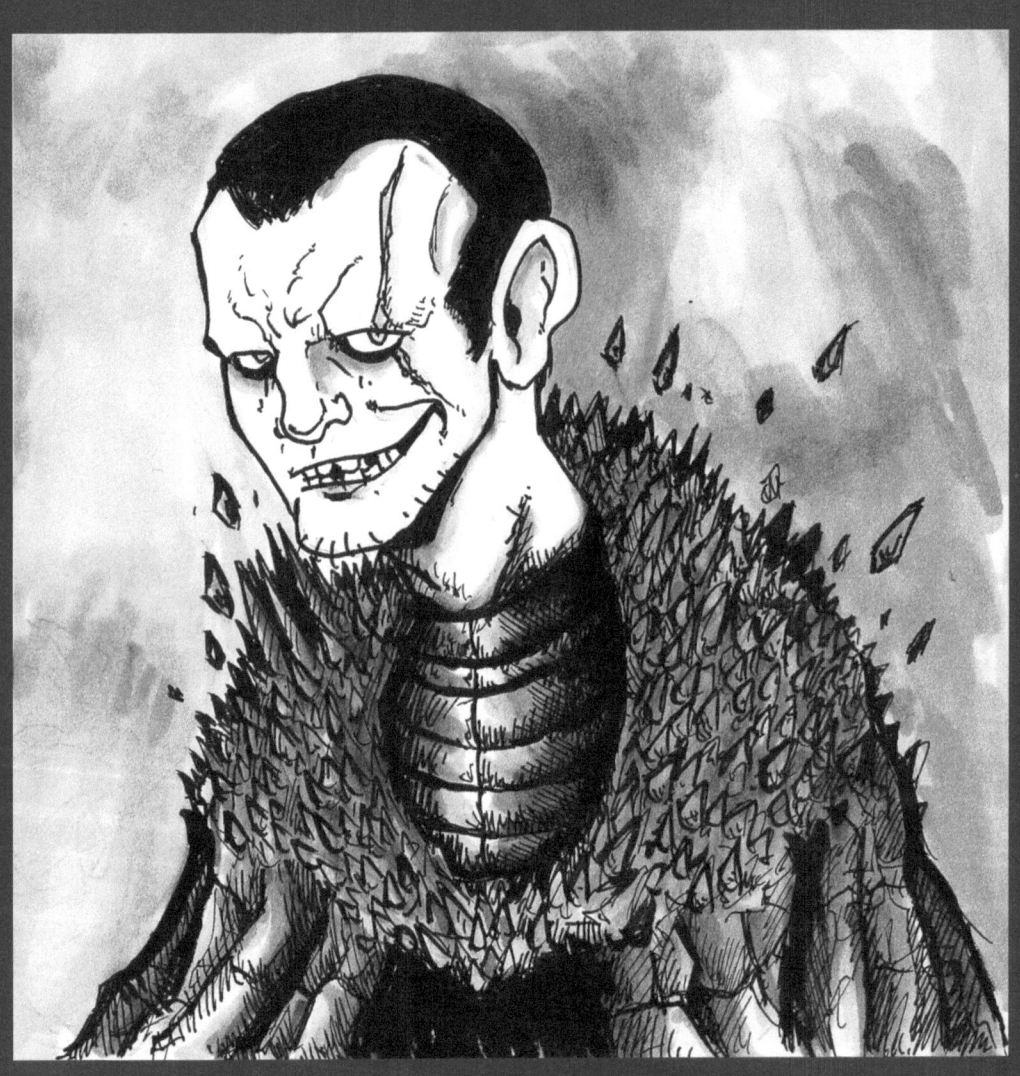

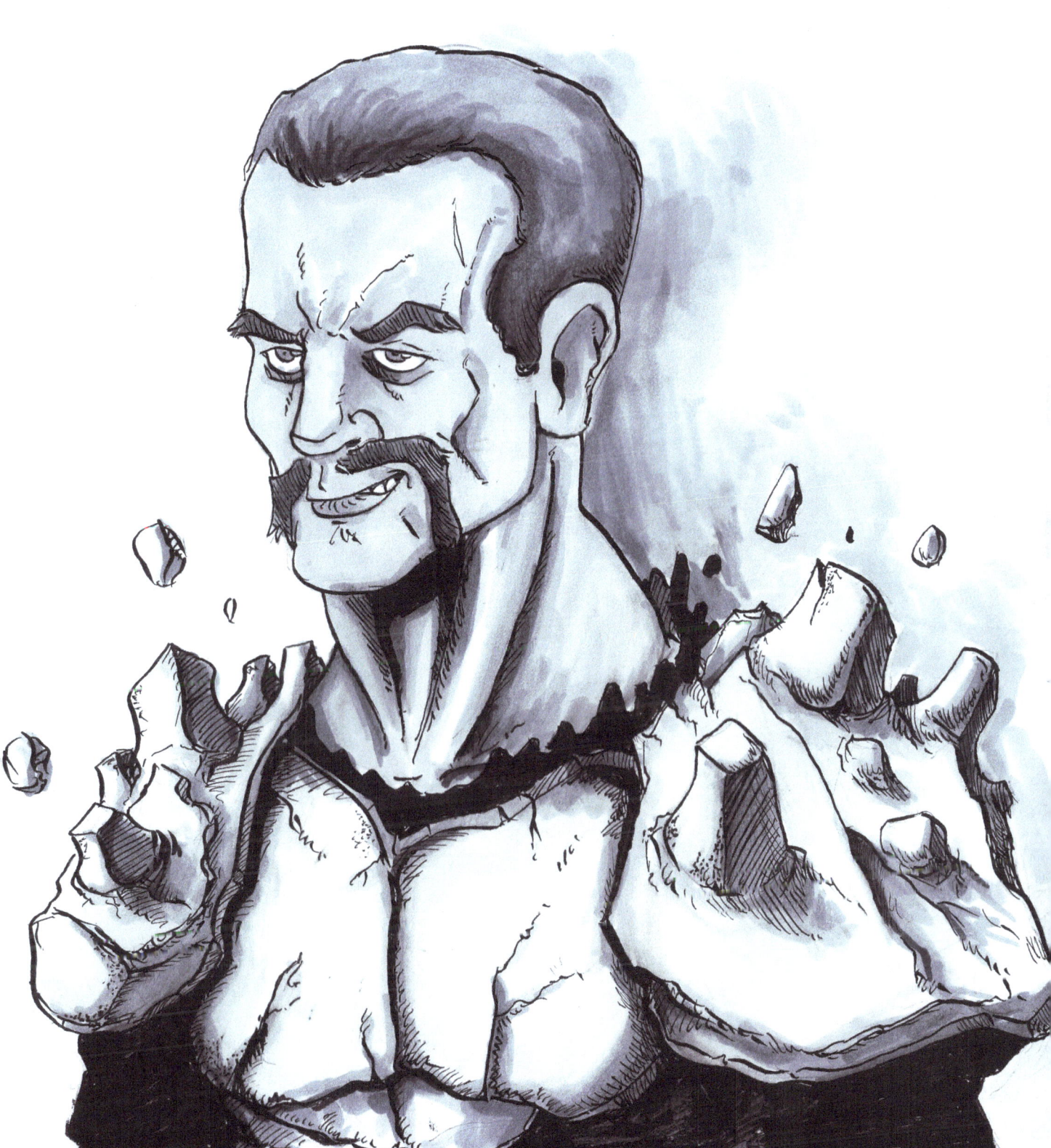

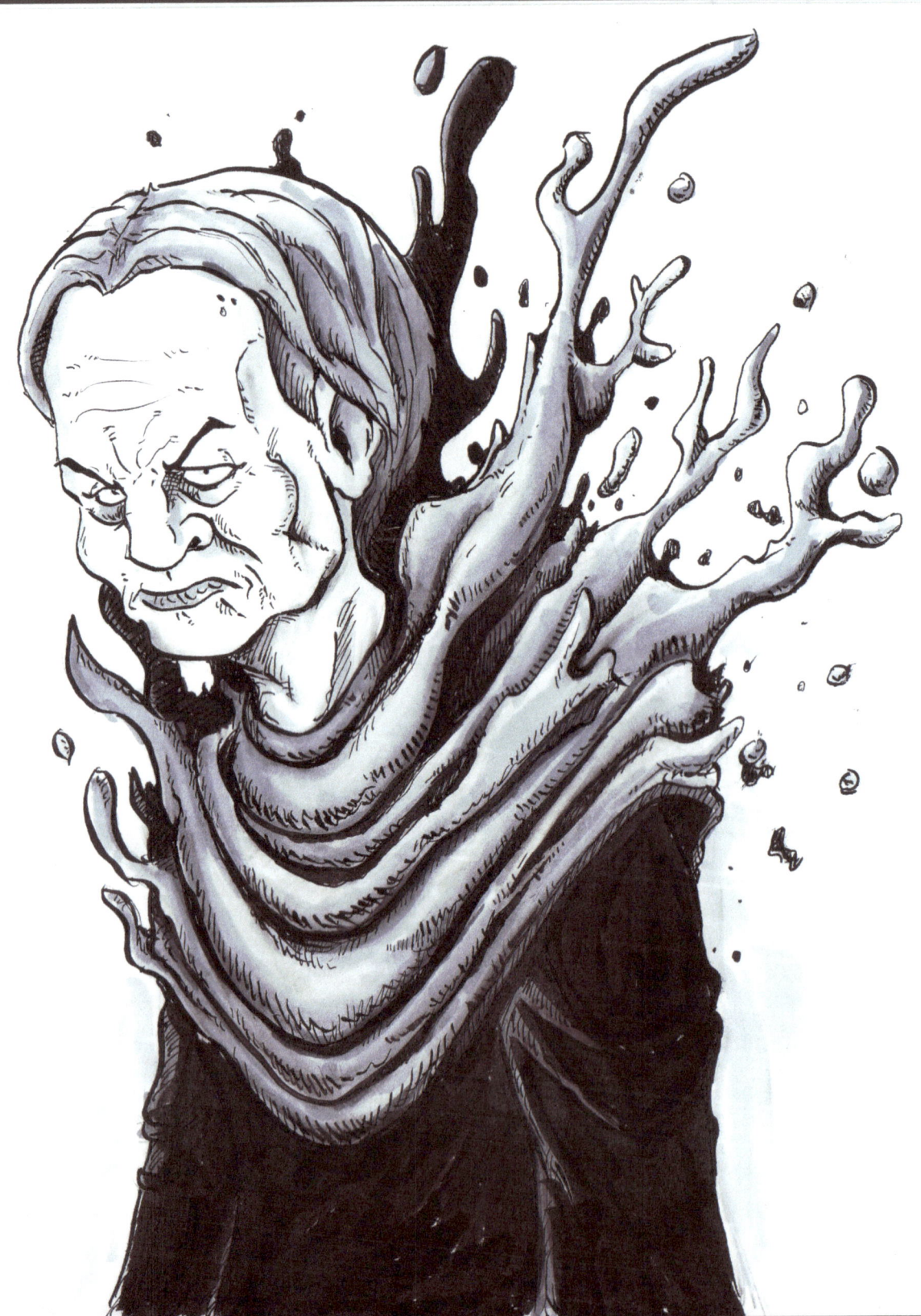

www.ingramcontent.com/pod-product-compliance
Lightning Source LLC
Chambersburg PA
CBHW050403180526
45159CB00005B/2137